WineFeast

Eat, Drink & Discover BC Wine

Copyright © 2010 by Troy Townsin and Cheryl-Lynn Townsin
Polyglot Publishing
www.polyglotpublishing.com

Food preparation, styling and photography by Gary Faessler
Cover design by Cassandra Whalen – caswhalen@yahoo.com

Printed in Canada by Transcontinental Printing

Library and Archives Canada Cataloguing in Publication

Townsin, Troy, 1975-
    Winefeast : eat, drink & discover BC wine / Troy
Townsin, Cheryl-Lynn Townsin.

Includes index.
ISBN 978-0-9737748-5-6

    1. Cookery (Wine). 2. Wineries--British
Columbia--Guidebooks. 3. Wine and wine
making--British Columbia. I. Townsin,
Cheryl-Lynn, 1979- II. Title.

TX726.T698 2009   641.6'22   C2009-905924-X

HOW CAN WE IMPROVE?

We strive for excellence and we value any feedback that will help us to make our books
better. We would love to hear your suggestions, and if you come across any information
that is out of date we'd appreciate you letting us know so that we can amend future
editions. Please feel free to tell us which recipes you like so we can keep the book
chockfull of your favourites. You can email us at contactus@polyglotpublishing.com.

WineFeast

Eat, Drink & Discover BC Wine

By Troy and Cheryl-Lynn Townsin
Polyglot Publishing

ALSO BY TROY & CHERYL-LYNN TOWNSIN
Cooking with BC Wine: A guide to the wineries of British Columbia
Cooking with the Wines of Washington
Cooking with the Wines of Oregon

ALSO BY TROY TOWNSIN
A Moose in a Maple Tree: The All-Canadian 12 Days of Christmas

Special Thanks

A special thanks to everyone who went out of their way to help us put this book together. It would not have been possible without your time, advice, and generosity. Of special note are Gary Faessler, Cassandra Whalen, Madelon Nagel, Alison Nagel and especially Ingrid Murray, who spent countless hours cooking, tasting and providing valuable culinary advice during the compilation of this book.

Others of special note are Russell and Deborah Fahlman of Kilrenny Farm in Cobble Hill, Scott and Katie Mahon of Mad Dog Crabs Fresh Seafood Market in Duncan and Neil Davis and Elizabeth Pungente of The Village Butcher in Oak Bay.

Contents

Introduction

BC wine has never been more popular and this is for a good reason. The wines of BC have won almost every major wine award in the world including Best Chardonnay Worldwide and Best Shiraz (London International Wine and Spirits Competition), World's Best Icewine (International Wine Challenge), Best in Class Meritage (LA County Fair) and countless Best of Varietal, Best of Class, Gold and Double Gold at competitions like Chardonnay Du Monde (France), Pacific Rim International (US), VinItaly (Italy) and many more.

But BC has a lot more to offer than just great wine. The spectacular scenery and incredible access to fresh local produce mean that in the culinary tourism stakes, British Columbia rivals any other destination in the world.

When our first book, *Cooking with BC Wine,* sold more than 10,000 copies and won a Gourmand World Cookbook Award, we knew we had done something right. This book stays true to the formula that made the first book such a success, but it is loaded with even more wine, food and travel information.

This book pays tribute to the wineries of BC with a collection of 150 recipes for cooking with wine. The majority of the recipes come from world-renowned chefs, winery owners and winemakers, who have disclosed their secrets, and in some cases invented entirely new creations, especially for this book. Others are our own personal favourites that we are pleased to share with you. The recipes feature easy-to-find ingredients and simple instructions. This book proves that you don't need to be a gourmet chef to cook like one. Each recipe has been tried and tested and we're sure you'll enjoy them.

One of the unique things about our books is that all of the recipes actually use wine as an ingredient. This is true wine-country cooking and as you work your way through the recipes in this book, you'll discover that cooking with wine is not only easy, it's also a fun, rewarding and social experience. This also means that you get to open a bottle of wine every time you cook; we almost called the book *150 Excuses to Open a Bottle of Wine.* We regularly employ the policy of a little wine for the food and a little for the chef.

We have laid this book out in sections beginning with information on cooking with wine and wine pairing. The two topics are actually related; cooking with wine can be the answer to all of your pairing problems. When matching wines with foods, we try to find flavours in the food that complement the flavours in the wine. Cooking with wine infuses the food with the flavours of the wine, so if you serve the same wine with your meal, you'll have a perfect match nearly every time.

You have the ingredients and you have the wine. This book will help you bring the two together. Some of the featured recipes are simple to prepare and can be whipped up after work using what you have in the pantry, while others are more intricate affairs for special occasions.

The recipes cater to a wide variety of tastes; however, keep in mind that they are there as guides for your own culinary adventures, and feel free to adjust, experiment and substitute to suit your needs or requirements.

The book also includes information on wine education. We explain the ritual of wine tasting and what to look for in a good wine, as well as ways to improve your sensory evaluation skills. We describe the many grape varietals that are found in British Columbia along with a history of how they came to be in BC.

In addition to being a food and wine book, this is a guide to all of BC's magnificent wineries. We provide maps, regional information and contact information for all of the wineries in the province, making touring a little easier.

Whether you live in BC, or are just passing through, we hope you get the chance to visit some of the spectacular wineries featured in this book. And when the touring is done, pop the cork (or unscrew the cap) on a fabulous bottle of BC wine and cook up an unforgettable *WineFeast!*

Food & Wine

Wine makes a symphony of a good meal.

Fernande Garvin

Why Cook with Wine?

Why cook with wine? We'd be rich if we had a dollar for every time we've heard that question. Here are our top three reasons why you should be cooking with wine.

1. Wine will make your food taste better!

Even chefs who don't drink wine acknowledge that wine is a valuable ingredient that gives a wonderful flavour to food. You don't have to use an expensive wine in your cooking, but always use good quality wine.

When wine is reduced under heat the flavours intensify and the addition of wine can mean the difference between a good meal and a great one.

2. It's a lot of fun!

A little wine for the food and a little for the chef! Turn on some music and enjoy a glass of wine while you cook. Invite your friends into the kitchen, pour them a glass and socialize while you work your culinary magic.

3. Wine can be good for your health!

When you cook with wine it gives the food so much great flavour that you will find yourself adding less salt.

Studies also show that wine is beneficial for the heart and that moderate consumption may lead to reduced risk of heart disease. Wine is a rich source of antioxidants and it can actually lead to reduced stress levels when enjoyed in moderation.

FAQs about Cooking with Wine

Do I need to use the wine that is featured in the recipe?

The majority of the recipes contained in this book come directly from winery chefs and winemakers. These recipes feature specific wines and were actually created using these wines. However, you can always substitute these wines for similar wines that you have access to. As long the wine is good quality, the recipe will likely be every bit as good.

Several recipes ask for specific varietals such as Chardonnay, while others ask for non-specific wines like red, white or late harvest. If we have specified a varietal, then that is because we feel that specific varietal adds something special to the recipe; although again, you can always try experimenting with different wines for different results.

How can I choose a wine to cook with?

When choosing a wine to cook with, remember the golden rule: you must never cook with a wine you wouldn't drink. Wine is a powerful ingredient and its flavours can completely alter the taste of the dish. When wine is reduced during the cooking process its flavours intensify, which is wonderful if the wine has good flavours, as the dish will become even more delicious. Problems only occur when you cook with poor quality or faulty wine, as the faults in the wine also intensify. A wine need not be expensive to be good quality.

Another way to choose a wine to cook with is to use the food pairing guide in the following section of this book. There you will find a list of common foods and the varietals that pair well with them. Of course, these are just suggestions and only you can decide which wines you like best with which foods. If you enjoy a wine pairing, no matter how unusual, then it is the right match for you.

If I cook with wine does the alcohol disappear?

During the cooking process the alcohol in wine is significantly reduced. However, it would require a lot of cooking time to completely remove all of the alcohol. So if your dinner guests can't consume any alcohol, it's safer not to serve them food cooked with wine.

According to a study conducted by the US Department of Agriculture, after about 15 minutes of simmering or baking only 40% of the alcohol remains. After an hour it is reduced to about 25%. After simmering or baking for 2.5 hours there would only be about 5% of the alcohol left in the dish.

Can I use cooking wine instead?

NO! Never put anything labelled "cooking wine" in your food. These wines are full of vinegars, salts and chemicals and they can ruin the flavour of your dish. If you wouldn't like to drink it, then don't cook with it. It is our honest opinion that the results would be better using no wine than using cooking wine.

If you are cooking for someone who can't consume any alcohol, you still have a few options. If the recipe calls for stock, then you could try replacing the wine with more stock, or in marinades or dressings you could try substituting the wine with a little fruit juice. In some cases, you could just leave the wine out altogether. However, with any of these alterations the results will be different.

The authors enjoying good company and a harvest feast in the vineyard at Muse Winery

George and Trudy Heiss of Gray Monk Estate Winery sharing a joke over a glass of wine

What can I do with the rest of the bottle?

When you cook with wine, you are infusing the flavours of the wine into the food. So if you serve the rest of the bottle with the meal, then you will usually get a perfect wine pairing, as the flavours in the food and wine will now match.

If you don't want to drink the rest of the wine you do have a few options. If you've only used a little of the wine, you could re-cork it and save it for another day. Wine will last around 3 days in the fridge before it deteriorates rapidly. You could also use the leftover wine as a marinade for meats and fish or you could make wine jelly; some fabulous recipes for these are included in this book.

Some people will pour the wine into an ice cube tray, freeze it and then use the cubes at a later date to flavour sauces. This is not actually recommended, as the wine quality dissipates during the freezing process, but it can certainly be done. Just be sure to use a covered ice tray, otherwise the wine will absorb all sorts of smells and flavours from the freezer.

Food & Wine Pairing

Pairing food and wine can seem intimidating at times. Fortunately, as long as you have great wine and delicious food, even if you don't get the ideal combination every time, it's still a lot of fun trying. By analysing each pairing while eating, you can always learn lessons for next time. Here are some common foods and a few wine pairing tips that will help you find that perfect match.

Asian Cuisine Traditionally, (grape) wine isn't served with Asian cuisine and in many Asian countries wine is only just beginning to catch on. However, there are some incredible wine matches for those of us who do enjoy a glass of wine with our Asian dishes.

Lighter, aromatic wines are usually a top choice for Asian cuisine; Riesling, Gewürztraminer and Chenin Blanc all make great accompaniments to most dishes as the exotic aromas and hints of spice stand up nicely to the strong flavours found in curries or spicy foods.

With Japanese dishes such as sushi or tempura, sparkling wine is a wise choice. The bubbles work to refresh the palate after eating raw fish and they also cut through the grease in tempura batter. Or, if you want to stick with the traditional, BC has its own sake producer located on Granville Island.

Red wines are harder to pair with Asian cuisine because the tannins can be a bit overpowering, but a lighter style red such as Pinot Noir or Rosé can work very well.

Beef It's probably no surprise that red wines are best for pairing with beef. For barbecues, Syrah (Shiraz) is a great choice as the peppery, sometimes smoky, characteristics of the varietal make a great match with grilled meat.

Bordeaux varietals on their own (Cabernet Sauvignon, Merlot, Cabernet Franc, Malbec and Petit Verdot) are an excellent choice with steak. With roast beef, the Bordeaux-style blends (Meritage) are hard to beat.

The cut of meat is also something to consider when pairing wine with beef. For example, Cabernet Sauvignon would be better suited to rib eye steak than sirloin, as fattier meats react very well with the higher tannins that are usually present in this varietal. Merlot and Syrah are both fantastic choices for tenderloin and sirloin steaks.

For white wine lovers, Chardonnay can be delicious paired with roast beef as both display full, rich flavours and Gewürztraminer is a top choice for a beef stir-fry, as it's spicy, fragrant and exotic.

Cheese Platters, Nibbles and Appetizers

It can be a daunting task selecting wines to go with a variety of appetizers. A great choice that is often overlooked is sparkling wine. This wine style is extremely food friendly and the bubbles cleanse the palate between bites. Deep-fried foods and salty foods that can be very difficult to pair are no problem for a bottle of bubbly.

White wines such as Gewürztraminer, Pinot Gris or Pinot Blanc are also good choices for appetizers as they tend to be light and food friendly. For reds stick with the lighter styles such as Rosé, Gamay Noir or Pinot Noir.

When choosing wines to go with cheese, white or fruit wines tend to work well with softer cheeses (Brie, Camembert). Sauvignon Blanc is an excellent match for goat cheese. Hard cheeses, such as aged Cheddars, pair equally well with red or white wines and Syrah, Cabernet Sauvignon and Merlot are all popular red choices while Gewürztraminer, Riesling and Pinot Gris are great white choices. Port-style wines are a fantastic match for blue cheeses.

Chocolate

It is actually very difficult to pair wine with chocolate. Fruit wines and port-style wines tend to work best and some great pairings can be made utilizing well-known flavour matches such as raspberry, blackberry and cherry with chocolate.

If you have good quality dark chocolate, then it's also possible to get a wonderful match with big reds that display cocoa characteristics, such as Cabernet Franc, Cabernet Sauvignon, or occasionally Syrah.

Desserts

When serving wine with dessert the most important rule to remember is that the wine should be sweeter than the food. This stops the wine from tasting dull. There are numerous dessert-style wines on the market and Botrytis-affected or late harvest wines are a good match for most desserts.

However, it is Icewine that has become the ultimate dessert wine. This amazing beverage makes a wonderful dessert on its own and need not be served with food to shine.

Lamb

Being a rich and succulent meat, lamb pairs beautifully with wines that display strong fruit characteristics. Pinot Noir is a good choice as the silky smooth texture and higher acidity make it a favourite match of many lamb connoisseurs. Shiraz is also a popular choice as the berry fruit and pepper qualities complement the juicy meat. If you are serving lamb with mint sauce it makes the match trickier, but Cabernet Sauvignon can work as it too sometimes has that hint of mintiness.

For whites, Chardonnay tends to have strong enough flavours to stand up to lamb, as does Riesling, especially if you are serving lamb in a stir-fry or a kebab with a yoghurt dressing.

Pizza and Pasta In most pizza and pasta dishes, the main ingredients are tomato sauce and cheese. In Italy, Chianti (dominating varietal is Sangiovese) would usually be the wine of choice, but we do not have much Sangiovese growing in BC. Light to medium-bodied red wines are a good choice for tomato-based dishes and Merlot works well, as do most red wine blends. For whites, Sauvignon Blanc and Pinot Gris are excellent choices and those that have not been heavily oaked would be equally suitable for both tomato and cream-based pastas.

Poultry One of the wonderful things about pairing wines with birds is that both red and white wines can be equally successful matches. With red wines, try a varietal that is really low in tannins, as high tannins will dominate the white meat. Pinot Noir and Gamay Noir are both excellent choices. If you enjoy the dark meat on chicken or turkey, or if you are serving duck, goose or game birds, you may prefer a Pinot Noir or Gamay Noir from the southern Okanagan as these wines tend to be a bit bigger and darker than those from cooler climates.

Rosé is usually a safe bet and if you are looking for white wines, then Chardonnay, Pinot Blanc, Pinot Gris, Viognier and white blends are all fantastic choices. Poultry is one of the easiest meats to pair successfully with white wine, so as long as you choose a good quality wine you should have plenty of success. If you are roasting a bird then you may like to choose a wine that has been aged in oak as the added complexity of these wines tends to match up very well with crispy chicken skin.

Salmon (also Tuna or Swordfish) Salmon is one of the fish that blows away the myth about only serving white wines with fish. Lighter style Pinot Noir from cooler climate regions make a wonderful match for salmon. However, just because there is a great match with red wine, don't discount the whites. Pinot Gris is another winner for salmon and the crisp, fresh flavours of this varietal are hard to beat. Dry Riesling and Pinot Blanc are also excellent choices.

Shellfish With Dungeness crab, prawns, oysters, mussels and clams, we really are spoiled in BC with our bounty from the sea. Sauvignon Blanc with fresh crab or prawns is very hard to beat and unoaked Chardonnay is also a good choice. Sparkling wines are excellent as the bubbles complement the delicate flesh of the shellfish. A Dungeness crab eggs benny with a glass of BC bubbly is a match made in heaven.

If the dish has some cream or cheese (such as crab cannelloni or prawn linguine) then a Pinot Gris or Viognier would be a great selection.

Except for Rosé or Pinot Noir, red wines generally do not work well with shellfish as their tannins can be overpowering.

Vegetarian Cuisine Wine is great with vegetarian food and reds are just as popular as whites. It is best to think of the weight or hardiness of the food when deciding which types of wines to pair with which foods. Hearty fare, such as vegetarian lasagne, bean burritos or eggplant parmigiana will have no problem standing up to bigger red wines such as Cabernet Sauvignon or Syrah. Mushroom dishes are divine with Pinot Noir or Chardonnay and dishes with goat cheese are fabulous with Sauvignon Blanc.

White Fish (Halibut, Ling Cod, etc.) The old white wine with fish rule was created in Europe at a time when cod was the only real table fish. Although we now know better, the rule is much more relevant to these white-fleshed fish and red wines should probably be avoided if you want the best match. If you are cooking a creamy dish, then a Chardonnay is hard to top. With grilled fish, Pinot Gris always shines and for pan-fried fish, a crisp Sauvignon Blanc will cut right through the grease.

If you absolutely must have a red, then go for something with less tannins, such as a Pinot Noir, to avoid the metallic taste that sometimes occurs when tannins react with the delicate flesh of white fish.

Wild Meat Hunting is very popular in British Columbia and wild meats such as deer, moose, elk or duck go very well with wine. The rich flavours in the meat pair well with the rich flavours in the wines. For red wines Gamay, Foch and Pinot Noir are excellent matches. Some top choices for white wines include Chardonnay or Riesling.

Appetizers

This wine is too good for toast drinking my dear. You don't want to mix up emotions with a wine like that. You lose the taste.

Count Mippipopolous in The Sun also Rises, *by Ernest Hemmingway*

Black Widow's Coquilles St. Jacques

Featuring Black Widow Winery Pinot Gris

Winemaker Dick Lancaster recreated this dish for his wife Shona after she fell in love with it while they were vacationing in Carmel. After a few trials he perfected it and it is now served as a much anticipated Christmas eve tradition. Luckily you don't have to wait until Christmas to try this recipe as there are scallops available year-round in BC. The lively acidity of Pinot Gris pairs extremely well with the richness of the seafood and cheese.

Serves 4

INGREDIENTS

1 bay leaf
¼ tsp thyme
1 tsp coarsely chopped parsley
3 tbsp coarsely chopped green onion
¾ lb scallops (if large, cut in half)
1½ cups Pinot Gris
⅓ cup water
1 tsp sea salt
4½ tbsp butter

½ lb mushrooms, sliced
⅓ cup half-and-half cream
2 egg yolks
¼ cup all-purpose flour
½ cup milk (1% fat or higher)
¼ lb cooked shrimp or small prawns
juice from 1 lemon
⅓ lb Gruyère cheese, grated
lemon wedges and parsley for garnish

1. Create a bouquet garni by wrapping the herbs and green onion in cheesecloth and tying in a bundle. If you don't have cheesecloth, you could use fresh herbs with longer stems tied together with string.

2. Combine the scallops, wine, water, bouquet garni and salt in a saucepan over medium-high heat. Bring to a boil, then reduce the heat and simmer uncovered for about 5 minutes. Discard the bouquet garni, transfer the scallops to a dish and reserve the liquid for later use.

3. Heat 2 tbsp of butter in a frying pan over medium heat. Add the mushrooms and sauté until they are slightly golden, about 3-4 minutes. Set aside.

4. In a small bowl, beat together the cream and egg yolks with a fork and set aside for later use. In a small saucepan over medium heat, melt the remaining 2½ tbsp of butter. Add the flour and stir well to form a roux. Gradually add the milk, stirring constantly. Continue stirring and gradually add 1¼ cups of the reserved poaching liquid from step 2, followed by the egg yolk mixture. Just before it comes to a boil, reduce the heat to low and stir until thickened, approximately 5 minutes.

5. Preheat the broiler. Divide the scallops, shrimp and mushrooms among 4-5 individual ovenproof gratin dishes. Add a small amount of lemon juice to each dish and top with the cream sauce. Sprinkle the grated cheese on top. Place under the broiler until the cheese begins to brown and the contents are bubbling hot.

6. Place the gratin dishes on serving plates garnished with lemon and parsley. Serve with a crispy baguette butter, and a cold bottle of Black Widow Pinot Gris.

Thai Meatballs

These Thai-style meatballs are a wonderful change from the norm and the best part is that they are very easy to prepare. You could fry them in hot oil, but baking them is a healthier option and the results are just as tasty. You can find the Thai curry paste in the Asian section of the supermarket. You could also experiment with green or yellow curry paste for slightly different flavours.

Serves 6-8

INGREDIENTS

1½ lb ground beef
¼ cup white wine
1 egg
2 tbsp fish sauce
1½ tbsp lime juice

1 garlic clove, crushed
2 tsp red Thai curry paste
⅓ cup finely chopped cilantro
2 green onions, chopped finely
¼ tsp salt

1. Preheat the oven to 450°F. Place all of the ingredients in a bowl and mix very well with clean hands. Make sure that the curry paste is well distributed throughout the mixture.

2. With wet hands, form about 20 small meatballs, approximately 1½ inches.

3. Place the meatballs on a non-stick baking tray and bake for 20 minutes, or until cooked through. Serve immediately on their own or with a sweet chili sauce or peanut sauce for dipping.

Barbecued Pork Sliders

Mini burgers, or "sliders", are all the rage these days. They are easy to prepare and a platter is perfect for sharing. We use baguette slices rather than mini buns, as baguettes are easier to find. The meat patties can also be pan-fried or baked in a 425°F oven for about 20 minutes. If you want to get extra fancy, try topping each burger with a little piece of bacon and a fried quail egg!

Makes about 12 mini burgers

INGREDIENTS

1 lb ground pork
1 red onion, diced
¾ cup crushed saltine crackers
2 eggs, beaten
½ cup red wine
1 tsp garlic powder

1 tsp salt
¼ cup butter
1 baguette, sliced into 24 disks
12 small slices cheese
your favourite condiments and burger
   toppings

1. In a medium-sized bowl, combine the pork, onion, cracker crumbs, eggs, wine, garlic powder and salt. With wet hands, form the meat mixture into 12 balls a little smaller than a golf ball and then flatten them slightly into small patties. For the best results, cover and refrigerate for 1 hour to firm up before cooking.

2. Butter the baguette slices on one side, then place them on a preheated grill over medium heat, buttered side down, until the bottoms are golden brown. Set aside.

3. Place the patties on a hot grill and cook for about 3-4 minutes per side, or until cooked through. Once they have been flipped, top with the cheese slices and allow the cheese to melt.

4. While the meat is cooking, spread your favourite condiments on the unbuttered side of half of the baguette slices. Place the meat on top along with your favourite toppings. Top with another slice of baguette, buttered side up, and enjoy!

Vietnamese Lemongrass Chicken Wings

Lemongrass is one of those ingredients that many people love the flavour of but are afraid to cook with. It is actually very easy to use and it makes a fabulous subtle addition, not only to Asian dishes, but to all sorts of dishes that would normally use lemon juice. Bruising the lemongrass with a meat tenderizer or rolling pin helps to release the fragrant, flavourful oils.

Serves 4-6

INGREDIENTS

2 stalks lemongrass

2 garlic cloves, crushed

3 tbsp fish sauce

¼ cup sugar

¼ cup white wine

1½ lb chicken wings or drummettes

1 tbsp olive oil

1. Cut off the root end of the lemongrass and remove the tough outer leaves revealing the tender stalk (about 4-5 inches long). Pound the stalks with the flat side of a meat tenderizer or a rolling pin, then mince. You can use a food processor to mince the lemongrass if you have one.

2. In a large bowl, mix together the minced lemongrass, garlic, fish sauce, sugar and wine. Add the chicken and stir to coat, then cover and refrigerate for about 3 hours, stirring occasionally to coat the wings.

3. Heat the oil in a large frying pan with a tight-fitting lid over medium-high heat. Add the chicken to the pan, reserving the marinade, and allow to brown for about 5 minutes on each side.

4. Add the reserved marinade to the pan, making sure that there is no more than ¼ inch of liquid in the bottom of the pan. Bring to a boil, then cover the pan and reduce the heat allowing the chicken to simmer, stirring occasionally, for about 15-20 minutes, or until the chicken is cooked through and the liquid has simmered off.

5. Serve on a platter with lots of napkins and/or finger bowls as eating wings always gets messy!

Jackson-Triggs Party Pies

Featuring Jackson-Triggs Okanagan Estate SunRock Shiraz

The meat pie is an Aussie favourite and in Australia they are devoured on an almost daily basis. The party pie is a smaller version of the meat pie that is intended as a popular party snack. Jackson-Triggs Okanagan Estate winemaker Brooke Blair (an expat Aussie) shares the recipe for this incredible appetizer that is divine served with the spicy SunRock Shiraz.

Makes 24 party pies

INGREDIENTS

1 tbsp lard (or shortening, or oil)

1 onion, chopped

1 lb lean ground beef

2 tbsp Worcestershire sauce

2 tbsp soy sauce

2 tbsp Shiraz

1 tsp beef stock powder

1 cup water

¼ tsp ground allspice

3 tbsp cornstarch, dissolved in 3 tbsp water

24 x 3-inch round pastry tart shells

1 package puff pastry, thawed (14 oz)

1 egg yolk, lightly beaten

1. Preheat the oven to 375°F. Heat the lard in a large pan over medium heat and sauté the onion for 3-4 minutes, or until soft. Add the beef and cook until browned. Stir in the sauces, wine, stock powder, water and the allspice. Bring to a boil, then reduce to a simmer, covered, for 20 minutes. Stir the dissolved cornstarch into the filling mixture and continue stirring until the mixture boils and thickens. Remove from the heat and allow the mixture to cool.

2. Place the tart shells on a baking tray or two and bake them for 10-15 minutes, until golden brown. Allow them to cool and then spoon the cold filling into the tart shells.

3. Preheat the oven to 400°F. Roll out the puff pastry into sheets large enough to cut out 24 x 3-inch rounds. You can use a cookie cutter or the rim of a glass with a 3-inch diameter to cut out the rounds.

4. Brush the edges of the tart shell with a little egg yolk and then gently press the puff pastry tops in place on the pies. Trim the edges if necessary. Brush the pie tops with a little more egg yolk to help them brown in the oven. Make 2 small slits in the centre of each pie.

5. Bake the pies for 15-20 minutes or until lightly browned. The true Aussie way is to serve the pies hot, with ketchup or "tomato sauce" as Australians call it.

Prosciutto-Wrapped Scallops with a Balsamic Blackberry Sauce

Scallops wrapped in bacon are delicious, but this delightful alternative is classier, tastier, healthier and easier to make. Served with a balsamic blackberry wine sauce drizzled over top, these scallops make a very sophisticated appetizer. You can adjust the recipe by using smaller scallops and smaller pieces of prosciutto to make a whole platter of these scrumptious treats.

Serves 4-6

INGREDIENTS

4 slices prosciutto, cut in half lengthwise

8 large scallops

1 tbsp finely chopped shallots

2 tbsp balsamic vinegar

2 tbsp blackberry fortified wine

1 tsp brown sugar

freshly ground black pepper

⅓ cup olive oil

1. Preheat the oven to 375°F. Wrap a strip of prosciutto around each scallop and secure with a toothpick.

2. Put the scallops on a non-stick baking tray and place in the oven for 10-15 minutes, or until the scallops are slightly opalescent. Do not overcook the scallops.

3. Meanwhile, in a small bowl, whisk together the vinegar, wine and sugar until the sugar is dissolved. Add pepper if desired. While whisking rapidly, slowly add the olive oil until thickened.

4. Plate the hot scallops, drizzle the sauce over top and serve immediately.

Caprese Salad Skewers with a Red Wine Vinaigrette

These attractive and delicious skewers are sure to be a hit at any gathering or event. The Caprese salad was invented in Italy, on the Isle of Capri, during the 1950s. Titina Costanzo invented the dish so that local women could "have a nice lunch and still fit into their bikinis." We think she would approve of this modernized appetizer version of her invention.

Makes 24 skewers

INGREDIENTS

1 small garlic clove

¼ tsp salt

1 tbsp dry white wine

½ tbsp lemon juice

1 tbsp balsamic vinegar

½ tsp sugar

2 tbsp olive oil

24 grape or cherry tomatoes

24 basil leaves

24 mini bocconcini or mozzarella balls
  (similar size to the tomatoes)

1. Use the back of a spoon to mash the garlic and salt in a small bowl. Add the wine, lemon juice, vinegar and sugar and whisk until the sugar dissolves. While whisking rapidly, slowly add the oil until the dressing has thickened.

2. Thread the tomatoes onto toothpicks or skewers followed by a basil leaf (fold the leaf if it is large) and mini bocconcini.

3. Arrange the skewers laying horizontally on a platter and drizzle the dressing over top.

Satay Chicken Skewers with a Peanut Dipping Sauce

These juicy chicken skewers, marinated in a wine dressing, are divine served with this tasty coconut peanut dipping sauce. A satay infusion that combines the best flavours of Asia in one dish on a stick. Satay is traditionally prepared on a grill, but you could also use a frying pan with similar cooking times.

Makes 24 skewers

INGREDIENTS

4 boneless, skinless chicken breasts

¼ cup white wine

2 tbsp lemon juice

1 garlic clove, crushed

3 tbsp soy sauce

½ cup peanut butter

½ tsp red pepper flakes

2 tbsp white wine vinegar

¼ cup coconut milk

1. If you're using wooden or bamboo skewers, presoak them in water for about 20 minutes so they don't burn on the grill. Cut each chicken breast into about 6 strips.

2. Combine the wine, lemon juice, garlic and 2 tbsp of soy sauce in a resealable plastic bag or a covered non-reactive dish. Add the chicken, ensure it is well coated and refrigerate for at least 1 hour.

3. Make the dipping sauce by combining the peanut butter, red pepper flakes, vinegar, coconut milk and the remaining 1 tbsp of soy sauce in a small saucepan over medium heat. When it is hot, remove from the heat and keep warm.

4. Preheat the grill to medium-high. Thread the chicken onto the skewers, working the skewer in and out of the meat so that it stays in place while grilling. Grill for 3-5 minutes on each side or until cooked through. Do not overcook and keep an eye on them to avoid burning.

5. Serve with the peanut dipping sauce and watch them disappear in no time.

Lotusland Vineyards Steamed Mussels in Pinot Noir and Garlic

Featuring Lotusland Vineyards Pinot Noir

Mussels make a wonderful appetizer or main and although they look impressive, they are very simple to prepare. In this delightful dish, the simple, fresh and clean flavours of the seafood shine through, complementing the delicate Pinot Noir and proving that a red wine can be paired successfully with delicate seafoods. The wine, garlic and tomato broth begs to be mopped up with crusty bread.

Serves 4-5

INGREDIENTS

36 live mussels

1 tbsp olive oil

1 head garlic, minced

1 can diced tomatoes, drained (28 oz)

2 tsp sugar

salt and freshly ground black pepper

1 cup Pinot Noir

½ cup chopped fresh parsley

lemon wedges for garnish

1. Discard any mussels that have damaged shells or that will not close when you tap them gently against the counter. Scrub the mussels and remove the beards by tearing them out of the shell. Rinse the mussels under clean running water.

2. Heat the oil in a large, heavy-bottomed pan with a lid over medium-high heat. Add the garlic, tomatoes, sugar and a little salt and pepper and sauté for 1-2 minutes before adding the wine. Bring to a boil, then add the mussels and ¼ cup of parsley. Cover with the lid and steam for about 3-4 minutes, until the mussels open. Discard any mussels that have not opened.

3. Remove from the heat. Taste the sauce and add more salt and pepper if necessary. Garnish with the lemon wedges and the remaining ¼ cup of parsley. Serve with crusty bread to soak up the broth.

Lake Breeze Pinotage Poached Pears Stuffed with Blue Cheese

Featuring Lake Breeze Vineyard Seven Poplars Pinotage

This recipe is a favourite of Chef Genevieve deVries of Lake Breeze Vineyards. She was inspired by an Italian neighbour in her hometown of Smithers, who made red wine poached pears as a dessert, served with gelato. Genevieve adapted the recipe, adding the blue cheese and walnuts, to create this amazing appetizer. The warm spice flavours of the Seven Poplars Pinotage pair beautifully with this dish. For less intense flavour, you can replace some of the wine with water.

Serves 4

INGREDIENTS

3 cups Pinotage (or other spicy red wine)

4 tsp whole black peppercorns

1 vanilla bean, split and scraped

3 tbsp grated orange zest

6 cloves

1½ cups sugar

4 ripe pears, peeled

½ cup blue cheese, crumbled

¼ cup toasted walnuts

honey for garnish (optional)

1. Place the wine, peppercorns, vanilla bean, 2 tbsp of zest, cloves and sugar in a saucepan that is just big enough to hold all the pears. Cook over medium-high heat, stirring occasionally, until the sugar is dissolved. Bring to a boil, then reduce to a gentle simmer. Place the pears in the saucepan and cook, turning occasionally, for about 30-45 minutes, or until the pears are tender.

2. Transfer the pears to a plate and set aside, allowing them to cool completely. While the pears are cooling, strain the poaching liquid and discard the solids. Return the liquid to the pan, increase the heat to medium-high and reduce to a syrup, about 20-30 minutes. You should have about ½ cup of syrup left. Set aside.

3. When the pears are cool enough to handle, remove the inner core from the bottom of the pear using a melon baller or small spoon. Stuff each pear with 2 tbsp of blue cheese. To serve, pour about 2 tbsp of the poaching syrup on a chilled appetizer plate, then place a pear in the centre of the plate, with the filled end down. Sprinkle toasted walnuts around the plate and garnish with the remaining tbsp of orange zest. Drizzle with honey, if desired.

Prawn Pâté

If you are looking for an elegant dish to bring to a party, or to serve before dinner, then this is your winner. Easy to spread and full of flavour, this simple West Coast inspired pâté is sure to please. You can use any type of prawns, but BC spot prawns are definitely our favourite choice.

Serves 8-12

INGREDIENTS

2 tbsp butter	1 package cream cheese (8 oz)
¼ cup chopped onion	1 tsp Worcestershire sauce
2 garlic cloves, minced	6 drops Tabasco sauce
¼ cup white wine	½ tsp liquid smoke (optional)
1 cup peeled prawns	salt and freshly ground black pepper

1. Add ½ tbsp of the butter to a frying pan over medium heat. Sauté the onion and garlic until they soften and then add the wine. Bring to a simmer, then add the prawns and cook for a few minutes, or until they turn opaque.

2. Remove the prawns with a slotted spoon and let them cool. Continue to simmer the sauce until it is reduced to about 3 tbsp of liquid.

3. In a food processor, combine the cream cheese, remaining 1½ tbsp of butter, prawns, Worcestershire sauce, Tabasco, liquid smoke and the reduced wine sauce. Blend until smooth. Adjust the flavour with salt and pepper and additional Tabasco and/or liquid smoke if desired.

4. Transfer the dip to a small dish and refrigerate for 2 hours before serving. Serve with Melba rounds or crackers of your choice.

Domaine de Chaberton Compote d'Oignon aux Vin Rouge

Featuring Domaine de Chaberton Cuvee Rouge

Chef Ashley Chisham of Domaine de Chaberton's famed Bacchus Bistro has worked his magic to create this simple yet delicious onion compote. This dish makes a wonderful accompaniment for crackers and any type of pâté or cheese. It is also fantastic served as a side dish with steak. The Cuvee Rouge is a delicious blended wine that is perfect for enjoying with simple, hearty fare.

Serves 4-8

INGREDIENTS

2 large white onions, sliced

1¼ cups red wine

3 bay leaves

4 tsp honey

3 cloves

1 tsp salt

freshly ground black pepper

1 tbsp all-purpose flour

1. Combine all of the ingredients in a small saucepan over medium-high heat and bring to a boil.

2. Immediately reduce the heat to a simmer and allow the wine to reduce until the onions are soft and there is very little liquid left in the pan, about 30 minutes. Stir occasionally to ensure that the onions do not stick to the bottom of the pan.

3. Serve hot, cold or at room temperature with pâté and crackers.

Domaine de Chaberton Estate Winery in Langley

Appetizers

Elephant Island Seared Scallops with a Roast Garlic Apricot Sauce

Featuring Elephant Island Apricot Wine

This incredible recipe from Elephant Island uses their delicious fruit wine to create a flavourful apricot garlic beurre blanc to accompany seared scallops. This simple recipe is very adaptable and you can use different types of fruit wine to change the flavour completely.

Serves 6-8

INGREDIENTS

20 large scallops

salt and freshly ground black pepper

3½ tbsp unsalted butter

1 cup apricot wine

3 cloves roasted garlic, mashed

1. Season the scallops with salt and pepper. Heat a heavy-bottomed frying pan over medium-high heat and add ½ tbsp of butter. When the butter is hot, cook the scallops in batches of 6 or 7 at a time, depending on the size of the pan. Don't crowd the pan. Sear the scallops for a few minutes per side, until they are browned and firm to the touch. The inside of the scallop should be just slightly opalescent. Set the cooked scallops aside in a small dish.

2. Deglaze the pan by adding the wine and scraping up the brown bits from the bottom of the pan. Stir in the mashed garlic and cook until the liquid is reduced by half. Add the remaining 3 tbsp of butter in small amounts, stirring frequently, until the sauce is smooth and creamy. Add salt and pepper to taste.

3. Serve the scallops in a pool of sauce and accompany with a glass of chilled Elephant Island Apricot Wine or Elephant Island Apple Wine.

Roast Garlic

Roast garlic makes a delicious addition to many sauces, or it can be enjoyed with cheeses, bread or crackers. You can roast a single head or do a few at a time and store for later use.

Preheat the oven to 400°F. Peel the outer layers of skin from the garlic head leaving the whole head together and the skins on the individual cloves intact. With a sharp knife, cut the top off the head, slightly exposing the cloves. Place the head on a baking pan and drizzle a little olive oil over top. Bake for 25-30 minutes, or until the head feels soft when pressed. Remove from the oven and set aside to cool. To serve, squeeze the roasted garlic flesh from its skin.

Muse-Styled Gravlax

Featuring Muse Gewürztraminer

This rich and buttery cured salmon creation from Muse Winery pairs beautifully with the fruity, lychee flavour of their Gewürztraminer. This dish requires a day, or preferably two, of prep time to allow the salt to preserve the fish, but it is well worth the wait. Wrapped in plastic wrap and refrigerated, gravlax will keep for up to 1 week. This dish is cured and not cooked, so the salmon should be commercially frozen and thawed prior to using it, which will kill any possible parasites. A home freezer will not eliminate all risk of parasites.

Serves 6-8

INGREDIENTS

1½ lb boneless salmon fillet with
  the skin on
5 tbsp salt
4 tbsp sugar

1 tbsp Dijon mustard
½ cup white wine
juice from 2 lemons
1 large handful of fresh dill

1. Place the salmon fillet, skin side down, in a wide, shallow non-reactive dish.

2. Mix together the salt, sugar, mustard, wine, lemon juice and dill in a small bowl and spread the mixture over the salmon so that it is completely covered. Cover the dish with cling film and place in the fridge for 24-48 hours. The longer the fish is left to marinate, the saltier it will taste.

3. After 1-2 days, unwrap the cling film from the dish and remove the salmon. Carefully rinse the marinade off the salmon and gently pat dry with paper towel. Place the salmon on a carving board, flesh side up, and slice thin, diagonal slivers with an extremely sharp fillet knife.

4. Serve with buttered toast or dark, dense breads, such as pumpernickel. Gravlax is also delicious served on an open-faced bagel with cream cheese, capers and chopped red onions.

Hester Creek Pistachio and Goat Cheese-Stuffed Mushrooms and Figs

Featuring Hester Creek Estate Winery Pinot Blanc

Mushrooms and figs may not seem like natural partners, but in this case the combination, created by foodie Pauline Gagnon at Hester Creek, is inspiring. The cheese and pistachios fill out the flavours of the mushrooms and figs and the Hester Creek Pinot Blanc accentuates the nutty, fruity flavours, ensuring that they are not overwhelmed by the cheese. This dish also works well with blue cheese instead of goat cheese, or you can do some of each.

Serves 4-6

INGREDIENTS

12 small button mushrooms	⅓ cup shelled pistachio nuts
12 dried figs	2 garlic cloves, minced
1 cup white wine	¼ cup finely diced red onion
6 oz soft goat cheese	fresh herbs for garnish (optional)

1. Separate the mushroom stems from the caps, discarding the stems. Cut the stems off the figs and hollow out the centre with your finger.

2. Put the mushroom caps and figs in a steamer and steam for 5 minutes over 1 cup of boiling wine. Transfer the steamed mushrooms and figs to a cookie sheet and set aside. Reserve the remaining wine.

3. In a small bowl, blend the cheese and nuts together with a fork.

4. Combine the garlic, onion and ½ cup of the reserved wine in small saucepan over medium-high heat. Cook until the onions are translucent and the liquid has evaporated. Remove from the heat and add to the cheese-nut mixture.

5. Fill the figs and mushroom caps with the cheese mixture and place them under the broiler for 7-10 minutes. This dish looks fabulous served on a bed of fresh herbs.

Black Olive and Cheese Crostini

Crostini have become one of our favourite appies and they are a great "apertivo" with a glass of wine. These tasty little Italian snacks are actually fried with red wine in the pan. We first fry the baguette in butter until it is crispy before adding the wine to the pan to avoid making the toast soggy. Good quality olives are essential for the success of this dish.

Serves 4

INGREDIENTS

1 egg
2 tbsp whipping cream
1 cup grated Parmesan cheese
1 small garlic clove

½ cup black olives, pitted
10 baguette slices, about ½-inch thick
2 tbsp butter
¼ cup red wine

1. Combine the egg, cream, cheese, garlic and olives in a food processor or blender and blend until smooth, but slightly chunky, similar to the texture of pesto.

2. Spread the paste onto 1 side of each baguette slice.

3. Melt the butter in a large frying pan over medium heat. If your pan is not big enough to hold all of the baguette slices, divide the butter and do 2 batches. When the butter begins to bubble, add the baguette slices with the spread side facing up. Cook until golden brown on the bottom and then reduce the temperature to medium-low.

4. Remove the pan from the heat and carefully add the wine directly to the pan around the bread- not over top! Return the pan to the heat and cover. Cook for about 5 minutes, until the cheese has completely melted. Serve immediately.

Kalamata Red Wine Tapenade

Kalamata olives are perfect for making tapenade. It's best if you buy them with the pit in as you'll get more flavour from the olives if you take the time to remove the pits yourself. Buy good quality olives and you can't go wrong. The red wine gives the tapenade body and the addition of capers and anchovies makes the dish salty but incredibly tasty. This recipe only makes a small amount, but with such strong flavours you only need a little on the bread.

Serves 4

INGREDIENTS

1 cup Kalamata olives, pitted

2 large anchovy fillets

2 tbsp capers, rinsed

1 garlic clove

1 tbsp dried parsley (or ¼ cup fresh parsley)

2 tbsp extra virgin olive oil

2 tbsp red wine

1. Combine all of the ingredients in a food processer and blend until fairly smooth, but still slightly chunky. Some people like this dish with more olive oil than others so feel free to add more oil if you like.

2. For maximum flavour, let the dish sit in the refrigerator for a couple of hours before serving. Serve with crusty bread or pita.

Mt. Boucherie's Pan-Fried Crab Cakes with Citrus Mayonnaise

Featuring Mt. Boucherie Estate Winery Semillon

Crab cakes are a staple on menus across North America and this easy-to-make version is one of the best. If you have access to fresh Dungeness crabmeat then you should use it, but canned crabmeat also works very well. It is important to give the cakes time in the fridge to fuse together so they don't fall apart while cooking. The Mt. Boucherie Semillon makes a perfect accompaniment!

Serves 8-10

INGREDIENTS

1 lb cooked crabmeat

½ cup breadcrumbs

2 tbsp Dijon mustard

2 green onions, finely chopped

1 tbsp + 1½ tsp lemon juice

5 tbsp mayonnaise

1 tsp Worcestershire sauce

¼ cup dry white wine

1 egg, beaten

freshly ground black pepper

3 drops Tabasco sauce

2 tbsp butter

1. In a medium-sized bowl, combine the crabmeat, breadcrumbs, 1 tbsp of mustard, green onions, 1 tbsp of lemon juice, 1 tbsp of mayonnaise, Worcestershire sauce, wine, egg and a little pepper to taste and mix well.

2. With wet hands form the mixture into 8-10 large crab cakes and place them on a plate. Cover and refrigerate for at least one hour.

3. To make the dipping sauce, mix together the remaining 4 tbsp of mayonnaise, 1 tbsp of Dijon mustard, 1½ tsp of lemon juice and the Tabasco sauce in a small bowl. Cover and refrigerate until needed.

4. Melt the butter in a frying pan over medium heat. Add the crab cakes and cook until they are golden brown on each side, about 6 minutes in total. Serve the cakes immediately with a dollop of dipping sauce on the side.

Salads

A nickel will get you on the subway, but garlic and wine will get you a seat.

Old New York proverb

Blue Cheese Caesar

Everyone loves Caesar salads because of their strong, rich flavours. We take the classic recipe and turn it up a notch by incorporating blue cheese with a hint of white wine. You could serve this salad as a full meal on its own by adding a pound of cooked shrimp or slices of grilled chicken. If you don't need to serve such a large group, use less lettuce as the dressing will keep for a couple of days in the fridge, or longer if you don't use raw egg. The great thing about this salad is that it pairs equally well with red or white wine!

Serves 8-10

2 tbsp white wine
2 tbsp lemon juice
4 garlic cloves, minced
1 egg yolk (optional)
1 tbsp Dijon mustard
2 tsp Worcestershire sauce
6 anchovy fillets

freshly ground black pepper
1 cup olive oil
¼ cup crumbled blue cheese
6 tbsp freshly grated Parmesan
    cheese plus extra for garnish
2 heads of romaine lettuce, torn into
    bite-sized pieces

1. Put the wine, lemon juice, garlic, egg yolk, mustard, Worcestershire sauce, anchovies and a little pepper in a blender or food processor and blend until smooth. With the machine running, add the olive oil, in a thin, steady stream until all of the oil is incorporated.

2. Add the blue cheese and the Parmesan to the food processor and pulse until well combined. Put the dressing in a small non-reactive bowl, cover and refrigerate until needed.

3. Put the lettuce in a large bowl and toss with the dressing. Add the dressing in batches as you may not need all of it. Garnish with Parmesan cheese and serve with crusty French bread or toasted garlic bread. You could also add fresh croutons to the salad before tossing.

Perfect Croutons

2 tbsp butter or garlic butter
3 cups day-old bread, crusts removed and cut into ½-inch cubes
3 tbsp finely grated Parmesan cheese

1. Preheat the oven to 350°F. Melt the butter in a large frying pan over medium heat until it foams. Add the bread cubes and toss to coat with the melted butter. Immediately add the Parmesan cheese and toss well, melting the cheese slightly.

2. Transfer the croutons to a baking sheet and bake for about 15-20 minutes, until they are crisp and golden, but still soft inside. Check and turn occasionally. Add to the salad just before serving.

Roasted Parsnip and Apple Salad

Parsnips rarely get the attention that they deserve, especially since they contain more minerals and vitamins than their relative, the carrot. When they are roasted they become sweet and succulent and can be far superior in flavour to most carrots. This salad has a wonderful mixture of textures and flavours and it uses a spicy Riesling to tie them all together.

Serves 6-8

INGREDIENTS

3 medium parsnips, quartered
olive oil
salt and freshly ground black pepper
⅓ cup pine nuts
1 tsp sugar
2 tbsp apple cider vinegar
2 tbsp Riesling

½ tbsp Dijon mustard
1 small shallot, finely chopped
½ cup vegetable oil
5-6 large handfuls mixed baby greens
2 tart apples, cored, diced and
    sprinkled with lemon juice

1. Preheat the oven to 400°F. Toss the parsnips in olive oil and season them with salt and pepper. Roast the parsnips in the oven for 20-25 minutes or until golden brown and soft. Allow them to cool.

2. Heat a small dry frying pan over medium heat and lightly toast the pine nuts. Shake the pan until the pine nuts are golden brown, being careful not to burn them.

3. In a small bowl, mix together the sugar, vinegar, wine, mustard, shallot and a little salt and pepper. When the sugar has dissolved, slowly whisk in the oil and continue whisking until the dressing thickens.

4. In a salad bowl mix the baby greens, apples, parsnips and pine nuts. Add the dressing, toss and serve immediately.

Spiller's Nutty Spinach Salad with Sun-Dried Tomatoes and Feta

Featuring Spiller Apple Raspberry Wine

This attractive and delicious salad is tossed with a dressing created by Spiller's winemaker Laurent La Fuentes. It combines all sorts of mouth-watering flavours and textures. If you can't find the apple-raspberry wine, feel free to substitute for another of Laurent's delicious fruit wines.

Serves 4-6

INGREDIENTS

½ cup chopped almonds

¼ cup olive oil

2 tbsp fruit wine

¼ tsp ground black pepper

1 garlic clove, crushed

4 large handfuls baby spinach leaves

¼ cup sun-dried tomatoes, chopped

½ cup crumbled feta cheese

1. Place the nuts in a dry pan over medium heat. Stir frequently until lightly toasted, being careful not to burn them. The nuts will be aromatic and golden when done.

2. To make the dressing, whisk together the oil, fruit wine, pepper and garlic in a small bowl.

3. In a large bowl combine the spinach, almonds, sun-dried tomatoes, feta cheese and the dressing, toss and serve immediately.

Warm Potato Salad Fused with Wine and Herbs

This mayonnaise-free potato salad is full of flavour and makes a delicious, healthy change from the ordinary. There are lots of different ingredients that could be added to this salad and you could even make it into a meal in its own right. Some suggestions for additions are capers and smoked salmon, or crispy fried bacon and boiled eggs.

Serves 4-6

INGREDIENTS

2 lb Yukon Gold potatoes, cut into
 ¼-inch slices
¼ cup white wine
¼ cup olive oil
1 tbsp white wine vinegar
2 shallots, finely chopped

3 ribs celery, chopped
½ cup chopped fresh flat-leaf parsley
3 tbsp chopped fresh herbs (tarragon,
 dill, thyme, basil, etc.)
salt and freshly ground black pepper

1. Put the potatoes in a large pot and cover with salted water. Bring to a boil over high heat and then reduce the heat to medium. Simmer until the potatoes are just tender, about 5-7 minutes.

2. Drain the potatoes and transfer to a large bowl, then pour the wine over top of the cooling spuds. Allow them to soak up the wine for about 5 minutes. You may need to gently toss them after a couple of minutes to make sure they are all covered.

3. In a small bowl, mix together the olive oil, vinegar, shallots, celery, parsley and other herbs. Season to taste with salt and pepper, then add the dressing to the potatoes and gently toss. This potato salad is best served warm. You can serve immediately or allow to cool and serve at room temperature.

Merridale's Apple Cider Salad

Featuring Merridale Cyser Cider

This delicious dressing from Merridale Cidery contains both apple cider and apple cider vinegar, also made at the cidery. It is a great way to liven up any salad as the apple flavours infuse beautifully with the olive oil. By changing the types of greens in the salad or adding extra goodies, such as goat cheese or walnuts, you will dramatically alter the final outcome.

Serves 6-8

INGREDIENTS

¼ cup apple cider vinegar
1 tsp Dijon mustard
1 small garlic clove
1 tsp dried oregano
1 tsp honey

¾ cup olive oil
¼ cup apple cider
salt and freshly ground black pepper
1-2 tsp sugar (to taste)
6 large handfuls organic greens

1. Place the vinegar, mustard, garlic, oregano and honey in a blender or food processor and blend well. While blending, slowly add the oil and then thin down with the cider.

2. Taste the dressing and adjust with salt, pepper and a bit of sugar to taste. Mix well.

3. Divide the greens evenly among the plates. Drizzle with the apple cider dressing and serve immediately.

Apples ready to be picked at Merridale Estate Cidery in Cobble Hill

Broccoli, Cucumber and Bacon Crunch Salad

Broccoli is one of the tastiest vegetables and during the summer months it seems a shame to cook it. This simple recipe makes a great accompaniment to any barbecue dishes. If you are in a hurry, you could use precooked bacon, available in most supermarkets. If you are catering to vegetarians, substitute the bacon for some salted cashews so that you maintain the salty-sweet combination that works so well in this dish.

Serves 6-8

INGREDIENTS

½ lb bacon

2 large heads broccoli, chopped into small pieces

1 cucumber, chopped

1 red onion, finely chopped

2 tbsp white wine

1 tbsp white wine vinegar

2 tbsp sugar

1 cup mayonnaise

salt and freshly ground black pepper

½ cup sunflower seeds

1. Cook the bacon in a frying pan over medium heat, until crispy. Set aside to cool, then chop into small pieces.

2. In a large salad bowl, combine the broccoli, cucumber, onion and cooked bacon.

3. In a small bowl, combine the wine, vinegar, sugar and mayonnaise.

4. Add the dressing to the salad and stir through. Season with salt and pepper to taste. Cover and refrigerate until serving. Just before serving, add the sunflower seeds and stir through.

Greek Salad

Greek salad has become a worldwide favourite as a side dish, or as a meal in its own right. In Greece, it is often referred to as a "village salad" and it is usually served before the main meal. Olives and olive oil are perhaps the most prized of all the Greek crops and these key ingredients need to be good quality for a successful salad.

Serves 4-6

INGREDIENTS

1 garlic clove, crushed

½ tsp salt

2 tbsp red wine

1 tbsp lemon juice

2 tbsp chopped fresh oregano

¼ cup olive oil

1 cucumber, chopped

2 tomatoes, chopped

1 green pepper, chopped

1 small red onion, thinly sliced

1 cup kalamata olives

1 cup crumbled feta cheese

1. Mash the garlic and salt together in a small bowl using the back of a spoon. Add the wine, lemon juice and oregano. Slowly add the olive oil while whisking vigorously, until the mixture is well combined and thickened.

2. Combine the cucumber, tomatoes, green pepper, onion and olives in a large salad bowl. Pour the dressing over top and toss the salad gently. Let the salad marinate for about 30 minutes and then top with the feta cheese just before serving.

Edamame Sesame Salad

Edamame is actually the Japanese word for soybeans in the shell. Here we serve them out of the shell accompanied by carrots and a sesame dressing. This healthy salad, full of protein and fibre, makes a great side dish for any barbecue foods. We use fish sauce in the dressing; however, this can be removed when cooking for vegetarians.

Serves 4-6

INGREDIENTS

2 cups frozen shelled edamame

2 tbsp rice wine vinegar

2 tbsp white wine

2 tsp sesame oil

1 tsp fish sauce (optional)

1½ cups grated carrots

1. Cook the shelled edamame according to the directions on the package and allow to cool.

2. Make the dressing by combining the vinegar, wine, sesame oil and fish sauce in a small bowl.

3. Mix together the cooled edamame, grated carrots and the dressing and serve.

Thai Green Mango Salad with Beaufort Ortega Prawns

Featuring Beaufort Vineyard & Estate Winery Ortega

Beaufort Vineyard & Estate Winery created this variation of a classic Thai salad that combines sweet, sour, salty and spicy flavours into one light, crisp dish. With fresh prawns gently simmered in wine, this salad can be served as a starter or a main course. The tropical fruit flavours and spicy notes of the Ortega make it a natural choice for seafood of any kind.

Serves 4

INGREDIENTS

1 mango, as unripe as possible
¼ red onion, thinly sliced
¼ red pepper, thinly sliced
1 fresh carrot, sliced into thin strips
¼ cup chopped fresh cilantro
20 mint leaves, chopped
2 cups bean sprouts
1 tbsp fish sauce

1 tbsp brown sugar
1 tbsp lime juice
3 tbsp butter
1½ lb prawns, peeled
¼ cup Ortega
¼ cup chopped peanuts (or cashews)
sprinkle cayenne pepper

1. Cut off the pointed ends of the mango and stand it up on one end. Peel the mango and then cut off thin slices using a serrated knife. Cut the mango slices into thin strips.

2. In a large bowl, mix together the onion, red pepper, carrot, cilantro, mint and bean sprouts. Cover and place in the fridge.

3. To make the dressing, whisk together the fish sauce, brown sugar and lime juice in a small bowl. Set aside.

4. Heat the butter in a frying pan over medium heat. Lightly sear the prawns on both sides, then add the wine. Move the prawns around in the wine and simmer for just a few minutes, until they turn opaque. Set the prawns aside to cool.

5. Toast the nuts in a dry pan over medium heat until fragrant and golden brown. Set aside.

6. Remove the salad from the fridge and mix with the dressing. Add the prawns just before serving and garnish with the nuts and a sprinkle of cayenne pepper.

Tomato and Watermelon Salad with Basil and Toasted Almonds

This delightful summer salad combines the unlikely pairing of tomatoes with watermelon. Watermelon has always been a popular summer snack on its own, but now it's starting to make an appearance in soups and salads such as this one. To add an extra dimension, add some crumbled feta cheese as a pleasant contrast to the sweetness of the watermelon and the acidity of the tomato.

Serves 4-6

INGREDIENTS

½ tsp salt

2 tbsp chopped fresh basil

2 tbsp red wine

2 tbsp balsamic vinegar

2 tbsp olive oil

4 tomatoes, chopped into large pieces

4 lb seedless watermelon, cut into large pieces

¼ cup sliced almonds

1. In a large bowl, whisk together the salt, basil, wine and vinegar. Slowly drizzle in the oil while whisking vigorously.

2. Add the tomatoes and watermelon, stir well and allow to marinate at room temperature for about 10 minutes.

3. Toast the sliced almonds in a dry pan over medium-low heat for about 4-5 minutes, or until golden brown. Stir constantly to ensure they do not burn.

4. Sprinkle the almonds over the salad and serve immediately. This salad is best served at room temperature for optimum flavours.

Opposite: One of the many unique signs directing visitors towards a winery tasting room

Soups & Stews

When you ask one friend to dine,
Give him your best wine!
When you ask two,
The second best will do!

Henry Wadsworth Longfellow 1807-1882

Bonaparte Bend's Asian-Style Chicken and Corn Soup

Featuring Bonaparte Bend Apple Wine

Every day, travelers stop in at Bonaparte Bend Winery to enjoy one of their many funky soups. This Asian twist on a classic American soup has proved to be a real crowd pleaser. The apple table wine cuts nicely through the coconut milk and gives the soup a refreshing lift. This soup can also be made using leftover roast chicken or turkey. Just reduce the cooking time in step 2.

Serves 4

INGREDIENTS

1 lb corn kernels (frozen or canned)
1 can coconut milk (14 oz)
2 tbsp vegetable oil
4 garlic cloves, minced
2 tbsp minced ginger
½ tsp red pepper flakes

1 lb boneless, skinless chicken, diced
salt and freshly ground black pepper
1 cup chicken broth
1 cup apple table wine
1 lime, cut into wedges

1. Place the corn and coconut milk in a food processer or blender and blend until smooth. Set aside.

2. Heat the oil in a large pot over medium heat. Add the garlic, ginger, red pepper flakes, chicken, salt and pepper and sauté for about 6-10 minutes, until the chicken is cooked through.

3. Add the corn mixture to the pot, followed by the chicken broth and apple wine and bring to a simmer. Simmer for 15 minutes, then season with additional salt and pepper if necessary.

4. Transfer the soup to individual serving bowls and garnish with fresh lime wedges.

West Coast Clam Chowder

Clam chowder is one of those dishes that people love to order at a restaurant, but rarely take the time to make at home, unless it's canned. With this simple version, you can whip up a batch of delicious hot chowder from scratch in under an hour. We like to use fresh Manila clams, but if you are desperate you could substitute for 1 cup of precooked or canned clam meat; just skip the first 2 steps and proceed directly to step 3.

Serves 4

INGREDIENTS

2½ lb fresh live clams
1 tsp salt
1 tsp cornmeal
¾ cup white wine
¼ cup butter
1 onion, finely diced
2 ribs celery, finely diced
1 carrot, finely diced
2 garlic cloves, minced

3 tbsp all-purpose flour
2 cans clam juice (10 oz each)
2 red-skinned potatoes, cubed
1 cup corn kernels (fresh or frozen)
1 bay leaf
1 cup light cream
salt and freshly ground black pepper
2 tbsp chopped fresh parsley

1. Before using live clams, especially if you have dug them yourself, place them in a bucket or pot of fresh water with 1 tsp of salt and 1 tsp of cornmeal. Allow them to sit for 15 minutes and they will expel any sand or grit from inside the shell. If there is a lot of grit you may need to repeat this process 2-3 times.

2. Bring the wine to a boil in a large pot over medium-high heat. Add the clams and cook covered for a few minutes, until the clams have opened. Remove the clams from the pot, discarding any that didn't open and transfer the remaining wine to a dish for later use. Separate the clam meat from the shells and set it aside, disposing of the shells.

3. Return the empty pot to the heat, reduce the heat to medium and add the butter. When the butter is hot, add the onion, celery, carrot and garlic. Sauté until the vegetables begin to soften, about 6-8 minutes. Add the flour and stir thoroughly. Slowly add the reserved wine and the canned clam juice, stirring well. Allow the mixture to come to a boil before reducing the heat to a simmer.

4. Add the potatoes, corn and bay leaf and simmer for 15-20 minutes, until the potatoes are tender. Remove the bay leaf, then add the reserved clam meat and cream and stir through. Add salt and pepper to taste.

5. Allow the chowder to warm through before transferring it to individual serving bowls. Garnish with the chopped parsley and enjoy with some crusty bread or saltine crackers!

Broccoli and Aged Cheddar Soup

Once upon a time, some genius came up with the idea of combining broccoli and cheddar cheese in a soup. The addition of the cheese and cream takes away any bitterness from the broccoli, and the wine boosts the flavour profile even further. This soup appeals to both adults and children and it's a great way to convince stubborn kids, spouses, or even former US Presidents (George Bush Sr. publicly refused to eat broccoli) that broccoli doesn't belong in the "axis of evil".

Serves 6-8

INGREDIENTS

2½ lb broccoli, cut into 1-inch pieces
¼ cup butter
1 small onion, diced
¼ cup all-purpose flour
3½ cups vegetable stock (or chicken)

½ cup dry white wine
1 cup light cream
2 cups grated aged cheddar cheese
1 pinch of nutmeg
salt and freshly ground black pepper

1. Steam the broccoli over boiling water for 5-6 minutes, or until just tender. Do not overcook; the broccoli should be bright green in colour. As soon as the broccoli turns bright green, give it a rinse in cold water to stop the cooking process.

2. Melt the butter in a large saucepan over medium heat. Add the onions and sauté for 4-5 minutes, until soft. Stir in the flour and slowly add the stock and wine, stirring continuously. Simmer for about 5 minutes before adding the broccoli. Stir through, then remove from the heat and set aside to cool slightly.

3. In a blender or food processor, blend the soup in batches. If the soup is still hot, don't fill the blender more than half way and be sure to remove the centre of the blender lid to allow some steam to escape, or the top may blow off making a big mess.

4. Return the soup to the pot over low heat and stir in the cream, cheese and nutmeg. Season with salt and pepper to taste. Heat through and serve immediately accompanied with crusty bread.

Potato and Leek Soup

This wonderful, hearty soup will warm your bones on the coldest of winter days. Or, you can serve it as a chilled vichyssoise (pronounced vee-shee–swaz), a refreshing summer soup. The leeks give a wonderful flavour and don't discard the green tips, as they will work wonders if you are making any kind of stock. If you don't have a blender or food processor, then it is best to serve it warm. Just chop everything very fine and mash in the potatoes with a hand masher or fork.

Serves 6

INGREDIENTS

¼ cup butter

3 leeks, chopped (white part only)

2 garlic cloves, crushed

1 onion, chopped

5 cups vegetable stock (or chicken)

1 cup white wine

4 medium potatoes, peeled and cubed

1 bay leaf

1 cup half-and-half cream

salt and freshly ground black pepper

¼ tsp nutmeg

1. In a saucepan over medium heat, melt the butter. Add the leeks, garlic and onion and sauté for about 4 minutes, or until softened.

2. Add the stock, wine, potatoes and bay leaf and allow to cook for about 25 minutes, until the potatoes are completely tender. Remove the bay leaf, then transfer to a blender or food processor and blend until smooth. If the soup is still hot, don't fill the blender more than half way and be sure to remove the centre of the blender lid to allow some steam to escape, or the top may blow off making a big mess.

3. Return the soup to the saucepan and heat over medium-high heat. Just before it boils add the cream, then reduce the heat to medium-low and keep stirring until the soup reaches the desired temperature (if serving warm). Add salt and pepper to taste, transfer to individual serving bowls and sprinkle with nutmeg before serving.

4. If you are serving the dish chilled, then allow the soup to cool before transferring to the refrigerator to chill completely.

Hillside Estate Cioppino

Featuring Hillside Estate Pinot Gris

This dish is a delicious medley of West Coast fish and seafood, created by Chef Peter Young. Don't fret if you can't get all of the seafood ingredients; you can substitute for whatever is fresh in your area. Peter likes to spice up this Italian-style bouillabaisse broth with plenty of chili flakes, but you can add them to suit your taste or leave them out all together. Pinot Gris is a quintessential seafood wine; the bright fruit flavours mingled with the fresh seafood make for a true feast.

Serves 4

INGREDIENTS

2 tbsp olive oil

2 cloves roasted garlic (pg. 32)

1 small shallot, chopped

½ lb mixed vegetables, julienned
  (carrots, red onion, zucchini, red
  pepper, green pepper, fennel, etc.)

12 large prawns, peeled and deveined

8 medium-sized scallops

8 oz boneless, skinless salmon, diced

good pinch saffron

salt and ground white pepper

chili flakes to taste

1½ cups Pinot Gris

1 cup tomato sauce

20 mussels, washed and debearded

4 oz cooked baby shrimp

1. Heat the oil in a large pot over medium heat and sauté the garlic, shallot and vegetables for 3-4 minutes, or until slightly softened. Add the prawns, scallops and salmon and cook for 2-3 minutes. Add the saffron, then season with salt and white pepper. Add the chili flakes to suit your taste.

2. Add the wine and the tomato sauce. When the liquid reaches a boil, add the mussels. Cover the pan and reduce the heat to a simmer for about 5 minutes, or until the mussels have opened. Discard any mussels that have not opened. Add the baby shrimp and heat through.

3. Serve in large bowls with lots of crusty French bread or focaccia.

Julienned Vegetables

When you julienne vegetables, it means to cut them into thin strips that are square, like matchsticks. Start with a peeled vegetable. Cut it into 3-inch long sections. If the vegetable is circular, like a carrot or an onion, cut the edges flat. Then make a series of parallel, lengthways cuts before turning the food on its side and repeating the process. You should end up with vegetables cut into 3-inch long sticks that are about ⅛-inch square.

Mission Hill Heirloom Tomato Gazpacho with Chèvre

Featuring Mission Hill Family Estate Reserve Sauvignon Blanc

Gazpacho is a tomato-based Spanish soup that is served cold. This is one of Chef Michael Allemeier's favourite recipes for a hot summer's day. He uses field-ripened, Cascade tomatoes and Piccollo goat cheese from Carmelis Goat Cheese in Kelowna. Goat cheese, often referred to as "chèvre", is a perfect match for Sauvignon Blanc. The success of this dish relies on the tomatoes being in season and ripened on the vine.

Serves 4

INGREDIENTS

12 vine-ripened tomatoes	sea salt to taste
3-inch sprig fresh tarragon	1 small shallot, finely diced
½ cup extra virgin olive oil	1 small green pepper, finely diced
¼ cup Sauvignon Blanc	2 oz soft goat cheese

1. Bring a large pot of water to a boil. Using a sharp paring knife, remove the core of the tomatoes by inserting a knife very close to the stem, about 1 inch into the tomato, and cutting in a circle with the knife pointed inward. The core should come out cone shaped. Score the tomato tops. Prepare a large bowl of ice water and set aside close to the stove. Gently drop the tomatoes into the boiling water for 12-15 seconds, then quickly transfer them to the ice water. Leave the tomatoes in the ice bath until they are cold to the touch, then remove them and carefully blot dry.

2. Carefully peel the skin off the tomatoes with a sharp knife, starting with the split skin where the core was removed. Cut the tomatoes in half lengthwise and squeeze out the seeds, holding the cut side down to avoid making a mess.

3. Place the tomatoes and tarragon in a food mill and gently pass them through. Alternatively, you could use a food processor, or push the tomatoes through a sieve; however, the food mill is best as is doesn't pulverize the tomato and gives it a great texture.

4. Place the puréed tomatoes in a large bowl. Carefully whisk in the olive oil and wine, then add sea salt to taste. Fold in the diced shallot and green peppers.

5. Serve at once in individual soup bowls, garnish with the goat cheese and drizzle a little olive oil over top. If you refrigerate this soup, bring it up to room temperature before serving as the olive oil will harden in the fridge. Also, tomatoes are always more flavourful at room temperature.

Opposite: The Terrace restaurant at Mission Hill Family Estate Winery

Wine and Wonton Soup

Ever thought of swallowing a cloud? That is the translation of the word "wonton". As they float around in the soup they are said to resemble clouds. This delicious soup is made using wonton wrappers, which are usually found in the frozen food section of the supermarket. Wontons are simple to make and although the process can be a little fidgety and time consuming, it can also be rewarding. Pour yourself a glass of wine to sip while you work to make the process more enjoyable.

Serves 6

INGREDIENTS

½ lb ground pork

1 tsp cornstarch

1 tbsp soy sauce

3 tsp sesame oil

1 egg, beaten

1 cup finely chopped cabbage

½-inch piece ginger, grated

salt and freshly ground black pepper

40-50 wonton wrappers, thawed

¼ cup milk

5 cups chicken stock

2 cups dry white wine

3 green onions, chopped

1. In a large bowl, mix together the pork, cornstarch, soy sauce, 2 tsp of sesame oil, egg, cabbage, ginger and a little salt and pepper. Place in the fridge to rest for 30 minutes.

2. To make the wontons, lay out 10-15 wrappers at a time on the counter and spoon about ¾ tsp of the meat mixture on the centre of each wrapper. Using a pastry brush, brush the edges of the wonton wrappers with a little milk. Lift two opposite corners and press the edges firmly together to create a little triangle with the meat sealed inside. Take the left and right corners, with one corner overlapping the other and press firmly together.

3. Combine the stock, wine and remaining tsp of sesame oil in large pot and bring to a boil over medium-high heat. Using a slotted spoon, gently lower the wontons, one by one, into the boiling mixture. Make sure they don't stick to the bottom. After 3-4 minutes they should float. Use the slotted spoon to remove the floating wontons and place them in individual soup bowls.

4. Repeat the process until you have cooked all of the wontons. Pour the hot broth into the soup bowls covering the wontons, then top with the chopped green onions and serve immediately.

Chandra Estate's Curried Beef Stew

Featuring Chandra Estate Lemberger

Indian food has become an important part of Canada's multicultural culinary landscape and curry is a hallmark of Indian cuisine. A true curry is actually a blend of fabulous spices and no "curry powder" is used. The Chandra Estate Lemberger pairs beautifully with the beef curry as its spice holds up to the curry's spices so it is not overwhelmed. This dish is even better when reheated the next day.

Serves 8-10

INGREDIENTS

3 tbsp olive oil
2 large onions, diced
2 tsp salt
9 garlic cloves, diced
5 tsp cumin seeds
3 large tomatoes, diced
4 tbsp tomato paste
½ cup water

2 tsp cayenne pepper
2 tsp turmeric
3 tsp garam masala
3 lb sirloin beef, cubed and fat trimmed
3 medium potatoes, peeled and cubed
½-¾ cup spicy red wine
1 handful fresh cilantro, chopped

1. Heat a large stainless-steel pot over medium heat and add the oil. Once hot, add the onions and salt. Reduce the heat to medium-low and cover. Stir occasionally, allowing the onions to sweat and caramelize, approximately 15-20 minutes.

2. Add the garlic and cover for 5 minutes. Add the cumin and cook for a few minutes before adding the tomatoes, tomato paste and water. Cover and simmer for 5-7 minutes, stirring occasionally. The end result should be a liquefied paste. Add the cayenne, turmeric and garam masala and simmer for another 5 minutes on low. Using a blender or food processor, purée the sauce. If the sauce seems too thick add a little more water.

3. Increase the heat to medium-low, add the puréed sauce and beef and cook covered for 45 minutes, stirring occasionally. Add the potatoes and wine and cook for another 25 minutes, or until the potatoes are soft. Remove from the heat, top with cilantro, then cover and allow to sit for an hour at room temperature.

4. Gently reheat if necessary and serve with basmati rice, warm buttered naan (Indian flatbread) and a dollop of raita.

Raita

½ large English cucumber, grated
1 tsp cumin seeds
1 lb plain whole milk yogurt (1 large container)

1 tsp salt
1 tsp cayenne pepper
2 tsp garam masala

Squeeze the liquid out of the grated cucumber to reduce the moisture. In a dry pan over medium heat, toast the cumin seeds. In a medium-sized bowl, mix together all of the ingredients and chill before serving.

Winter at Vigneti Zanatta Winery & Vineyards

Zanatta's Winter Warming Beef Chili

Featuring Zanatta Pinot Nero

Beef chili is one of those winter dishes that everyone looks forward to coming home to. The key to a delicious chili is a long simmer, as this is when the flavours intertwine. The chili tastes even better the next day when it's reheated. This dish freezes very well so it's great for stocking up the freezer with ready-made meals for those cold nights when you just don't feel like cooking. Zanatta's complex, peppery Pinot Nero makes an ideal wine for this dish.

Serves 4-6

INGREDIENTS

1 tbsp olive oil
1 large onion, chopped
3 garlic cloves, crushed
1½ lb lean ground beef
1 cup red wine
1 can kidney beans, drained and rinsed (19 oz)
1 can diced tomatoes (28 oz)

1 can tomato paste (6 oz)
2 tbsp chili powder (or to taste)
1½ tsp beef stock powder
1 tsp ground cumin
1 tsp sugar
salt and freshly ground black pepper
2 cups fresh corn kernels

1. Heat the oil in a large pot over medium heat. Add the onion and sauté for 3-4 minutes, or until soft. Add the garlic and cook for another minute. Add the ground beef and cook for 3-4 minutes, or until no pink is remaining.

2. Add all of the remaining ingredients except the corn and bring to a boil. Reduce the heat, cover and simmer for a minimum of 1 hour. The longer it simmers the thicker it gets and the better it tastes. About 20 minutes prior to removing the chili from the heat, add the corn.

3. Serve with crusty garlic bread, rice, pasta, or spoon over a baked potato and top with cheese.

Creamy Butternut Squash Soup

Butternut squash soup is the perfect, healthy comfort food for cool fall afternoons. This version uses Pinot Noir to add an earthy complexity to the soup's flavour. You will also find that a glass of Pinot Noir with the soup is a perfect pairing. If you are watching your calories, just omit the cream as this soup gets plenty of creamy texture from the potatoes.

Serves 6

INGREDIENTS

2 tbsp butter

1½ lb butternut squash, peeled and
  cut into ½-inch cubes

2 medium potatoes, peeled and cut
  into ½-inch cubes

2 medium leeks, chopped

2 garlic cloves, chopped

4 cups vegetable stock

1 cup Pinot Noir

½ cup whipping cream

salt and freshly ground black pepper

2 tbsp chopped fresh chives

1. Melt the butter in a large pot over medium-high heat. Add the squash, potatoes, leeks and garlic and sauté for 3-4 minutes. Add the vegetable stock and wine and bring to a boil. Reduce the heat to a simmer for about 20 minutes, until the squash and potatoes are very soft. Remove from the heat and allow to cool slightly.

2. In batches, transfer to a food processor or blender and purée until smooth. Return the soup to the pot and warm over medium heat. Before it comes to a boil, stir in the cream and add salt and pepper to taste. Transfer to individual serving bowls, sprinkle with the chopped chives and serve with crusty buttered bread.

Rocky Creek's Beef Burgundy Stew

Featuring Rocky Creek Pinot Noir

This hearty beef stew, created by the folks at Rocky Creek Winery, is slow cooked to allow for full integration of the flavours of the ingredients and the wine. The key to a good beef burgundy stew is in the wine, so always use something tasty. Pinot Noir, the traditional red wine varietal from the Burgundy region of France, adds a wonderful complexity to this recipe and the remainder of the bottle will pair nicely with the cooked stew.

Serves 6

INGREDIENTS

2¼ lb stewing beef	1 tsp salt
¼ cup all-purpose flour	4 cloves
½ tsp pepper	1 bay leaf
2 tbsp oil	¼ tsp dried thyme
¾ cup chopped onion	¼ tsp dried marjoram
2 tbsp brandy (optional)	2 tbsp dried parsley
1 cup beef stock	8 oz mushrooms, sliced
1½ cups Pinot Noir	6 carrots, chopped

1. Preheat the oven to 250°F. Coat the meat with flour and pepper in a plastic bag.

2. Heat the oil in a large pan over medium-high heat. Sauté ¼ cup of chopped onion briefly, then add the meat in batches to brown. Transfer the browned meat to an ovenproof casserole.

3. Combine the brandy, beef stock, wine, salt and herbs in the frying pan over medium-high heat. Bring to a boil, scraping up any browned bits from the bottom of the pan and then pour the mixture over top of the meat in the casserole dish.

4. Add the mushrooms, carrots and the remaining ½ cup of chopped onion to the casserole. Bake for 3½ hours, checking occasionally to make sure the liquid is still covering the meat and vegetables. If it's not, add a touch more wine or beef stock. Serve with crusty bread and enjoy with a glass of Rocky Creek Pinot Noir.

Chef's Tip

For a thicker gravy, you can mix 2 tbsp of all-purpose flour with ¼ cup of water and stir until smooth. Add ½ cup of the hot liquid from the stew to the flour mixture, stirring well. Pour the mixture into the stew and mix thoroughly. Return the pan to the oven and bake for an additional 30 minutes.

La Frenz Shrimp Bisque

Featuring La Frenz Reserve Chardonnay

This is the classic French method for making rich and flavourful shrimp bisque. The cream in this luscious soup is a superb match for the La Frenz Reserve Chardonnay and the delicate shrimp flavour is enhanced through the addition of this elegant wine. People tend to order bisque at fancy restaurants, but it's easy to prepare at home by following these simple steps.

Serves 6-8

INGREDIENTS

1½ lb whole cooked shrimp
1½ tbsp vegetable oil
2 onions, halved and sliced
1 large carrot, sliced
2 ribs celery, sliced
8 cups water
1 tsp lemon juice + few drops to taste

2 tbsp tomato paste
bouquet garni
4 tbsp butter
⅓ cup all-purpose flour
½ cup Chardonnay
salt and white pepper
⅔ cup whipping cream

1. Remove the heads, shells and tails from the shrimp, reserving them for the stock. Chill the peeled shrimp in the refrigerator.

2. To make the shrimp stock, heat the oil in a large saucepan over high heat. Add the shrimp heads, shells and tails and cook, stirring frequently, until they start to brown. Reduce the heat to medium, then add the onions, carrot and celery and cook, stirring occasionally, until the onions soften, about 5 minutes. Add the water, 1 tsp of lemon juice, tomato paste and the bouquet garni. Bring the broth to a boil, then reduce the heat, cover and simmer gently for 25 minutes. Strain the broth through a sieve and discard the solids.

3. Melt the butter in a heavy saucepan over medium heat. Add the flour and stir well to form a roux. Cook until it turns golden, then slowly stir through the wine and about half of the shrimp stock, whisking vigorously until smooth. Whisk in the remaining stock. Season with salt and white pepper if desired. Reduce the heat, cover and simmer for 5 minutes, stirring frequently.

4. Strain the soup into a clean saucepan over medium heat. Add the cream and a few drops of lemon juice to taste, then stir in the reserved shrimp. Heat the soup through, stirring frequently, then serve immediately.

Bouquet Garni

A bouquet garni is a bundle of herbs that is used to add flavour to soups. Usually the herbs are tied together with string or wrapped in cheesecloth. The most common bouquet garni simply contains parsley, thyme and bay leaves, but you could also add other herbs such as basil, tarragon, rosemary and savory.

Howling Bluff Onion Soup

Featuring Howling Bluff Sauvignon Blanc

This is a great soup for curing those winter chills. It can be served as a main course for 4 people or a first course for 6-8. Winery owner Luke Smith created this hearty soup recipe to finish off an open bottle of Sauvignon Blanc and the results turned out to be spectacular. The Sauvignon Blanc adds a wonderful crispness to the onion soup. Of course, vegetarians can substitute the chicken stock for vegetable.

Serves 4

INGREDIENTS

1 tbsp olive oil
1 tbsp butter
6 large Mayan or red onions
2 garlic cloves, minced
8 cups chicken stock
½ cup Sauvignon Blanc

1 bay leaf
¼ tsp dried thyme
salt and freshly ground black pepper
4-8 slices French bread, toasted
1½ cups grated Gruyère cheese

1. Heat a large saucepan over medium-high heat. Add the oil and butter and then sauté the onions for about 30 minutes, until well browned. Stir frequently and don't worry if the onions burn slightly.

2. Add the garlic and sauté for 1 minute. Add the stock, wine, bay leaf and thyme, then cover and bring to a boil. Reduce the heat and let the soup simmer for 30 minutes. Season to taste with salt and pepper and discard the bay leaf.

3. Ladle the soup into ovenproof soup bowls, cover with a piece of toasted French bread and sprinkle with the cheese. Place the bowls under the broiler and carefully remove them when the cheese bubbles. Serve immediately and enjoy with a glass of Howling Bluff Sauvignon Blanc or even Pinot Noir.

Opposite: The spectacular Naramata Bench

Soups & Stews

Fish & Seafood

Red with meat, white with fish, except lox or herring.
Rosé with any endangered species or an ice-cream cone.

Richard Smith - Author of A Gentleman's Guide to Understanding Fine Wine

Tinhorn Creek's Trout with Pinot Gris

Featuring Tinhorn Creek Pinot Gris

This is a recipe from acclaimed Chef Manuel Ferreira, owner of Le Gavroche, whose incredible food adds another dimension to the Tinhorn Creek experience. This recipe takes some time, but the results are impressive and it's actually quite easy to do. Vine leaves can be purchased preserved at most supermarkets, or you can use fresh ones. This recipe makes a lot of sauce, so you can make up to 4 trout keeping the same sauce proportions.

Serves 2

INGREDIENTS

2 garlic cloves

¼ cup hazelnuts (preferably skinless)

6 black olives, pitted

3 tbsp olive oil

1 tsp capers

1 anchovy fillet

8 small tomatoes, sliced (grape or cherry tomatoes)

1 handful fresh basil, chopped

1 handful chives, chopped

salt and freshly ground black pepper

4 shallots, finely diced

juice from 2 small lemons

½ cup Pinot Gris

4 sprigs fresh thyme

6 peppercorns

2 bay leaves

1 head roasted garlic (pg. 32)

½ cup whipping cream

½ cup chilled butter, cubed

6-8 large vine leaves (if using fresh leaves remove the veins)

2 whole trout, butterflied (bones removed)

1. In a mortar dish, add the garlic, hazelnuts, olives, 1½ tbsp of olive oil, capers and anchovy. Using a pestle, crush until a paste-like consistency is achieved. If you don't have a mortar and pestle you can use a food processor.

2. In a medium-sized bowl, toss the tomatoes with half of the chopped basil, the remaining 1½ tbsp of olive oil, chives and salt and pepper to taste.

3. Preheat the oven to 350°F. To make the beurre blanc combine the shallots, lemon juice, wine, thyme, peppercorns, bay leaves, and roasted garlic in a small saucepan over medium-high heat. Bring to a boil and reduce until there are only 2 tbsp of liquid left. Reduce the heat to low and add the cream. Begin adding the butter, 1 cube at a time, whisking continuously. Strain through a fine mesh strainer. Taste and adjust the seasoning with salt and pepper. Cover and keep warm until ready to serve.

4. Making 2 identical portions, lay down 3-4 vine leaves (for each portion) overlapping each other. Place the trout in the center of the leaves, then cover each fish with half of the tomato mixture, remaining basil and the hazelnut paste. Tightly fold the vine leaves around the fish, then tuck each end in to make a sealed pocket. Place the fish on a baking tray and bake for 12-15 minutes, or longer for bigger fish.

5. With scissors, slice open the portions and unfold the vine leaves. Serve topped with the buerre blanc sauce and accompanied by fresh seasonal vegetables and a glass of Tinhorn Creek Pinot Gris.

Arrowleaf Cellar's Creamy Shrimp and Saffron Linguine

Featuring Arrowleaf Cellar's White Feather

Saffron is one of the most incredible ingredients on the planet. It is a spice, made from the stigma of the saffron crocus flower, that has been used in cooking for more than 3,000 years. It is said to have marvellous healing properties and it gives a rich gold colour to food. Arrowleaf Cellars use the blended White Feather to give a fruity kick to the shrimp linguine. You could use frozen cooked shrimp, just substitute them for fresh and they will thaw in the boiled stock mixture in step 2.

Serves 4

INGREDIENTS

¾ lb linguine

⅔ cup white wine

⅓ cup vegetable broth

3 cups large uncooked shrimp or
  prawns, shelled

1 tbsp butter

3-4 garlic cloves, minced

4 green onions, sliced

pinch of saffron powder

⅓ cup cream

salt and freshly ground black pepper

grated Parmesan cheese

1. Cook the pasta in plenty of salted water according to the instructions on the package.

2. Bring the wine and broth to a boil in a small saucepan over medium-high heat. Add the shrimp, cover and remove from the heat. Allow to rest a few minutes, until the shrimp are cooked, and then drain the shrimp, reserving the liquid for later use.

3. Next, melt the butter in large frying pan over medium heat. Add the garlic and green onions and sauté for about 1 minute. Add the reserved wine-stock liquid, increase the heat and reduce the liquid to ½ cup.

4. Stir in the saffron, cream and shrimp and add salt to taste. Toss the sauce with the linguine and heat everything through before removing from the heat. Cover and let stand for 5 minutes before serving.

5. Serve topped with freshly ground black pepper and Parmesan cheese.

Succulent Baked Halibut with Feta, Zucchini and Tomato

For centuries, the best fish dishes have been cooked with wine. In this recipe, we combine fresh halibut with the wonderful Mediterranean flavours of tomatoes, zucchini and feta cheese. The great thing about this dish is that it comes with a ready-made veggie side dish. This dish also works with other types of fish or you could even use chicken, although it's hard to beat the halibut.

Serves 4

INGREDIENTS

2 tbsp olive oil

1 small zucchini, diced

1 small red pepper, chopped

1 small onion, diced

1 garlic clove, crushed

½ cup dry white wine

3 tomatoes, diced

3 tbsp chopped fresh basil

1 tsp lemon pepper

2 tsp seasoning salt

4 halibut steaks (6-7 oz each)

½ cup crumbled feta cheese

salt and freshly ground black pepper

1. Preheat the oven to 450°F. Heat 1 tbsp of olive oil in a small saucepan over medium heat. Add the zucchini, red pepper, onion and garlic and sauté for 3-4 minutes before adding the wine, tomatoes and basil. Stir well, bring to a boil, then reduce the heat to low and simmer for a further 5 minutes. Remove from the heat and set aside.

2. Rub some lemon pepper and seasoning salt into each halibut steak. Using the remaining tbsp of olive oil, lightly grease a shallow baking dish. Lay the halibut steaks in the dish, cover with the zucchini mixture and top with the crumbled feta cheese.

3. Cover the dish with foil and bake for 9 minutes. Remove the foil and bake uncovered for another 8-12 minutes, or until the fish is just cooked. The exact time will vary depending on the size and shape of the fish steaks, but the fish should flake apart with a fork when done. Serve immediately with rice or garlic bread.

Gourmet Fish Tacos

Fish tacos are a simple way to enjoy Mexican cuisine without all of the heavy cheese and beans. Although if Tex-Mex is your thing, don't panic, these tacos are served with a tasty sour cream sauce and you can always add cheese to taste. This recipe can be made using pretty much any type of fish including halibut, snapper, cod, bass, even salmon or tuna. If you like your tacos spicy, look for a Riesling or Gewürztraminer that has some spicy characteristics to achieve a great wine match.

Serves 6

INGREDIENTS

2 tsp olive oil

1 jalapeño pepper, chopped (or more
   to taste)

1 red onion, chopped

2 garlic cloves, crushed

½ cup white wine

½ cup chicken stock (or vegetable)

2 large tomatoes, chopped

½ tsp ground cumin

1½ lb boneless, skinless fish fillets,
   chopped

salt and freshly ground black pepper

juice from 1 lime

¾ cup sour cream

12 soft tortillas or hard taco shells

½ cup chopped fresh cilantro

¼ head lettuce, chopped

1. Heat the oil in a large pan over medium heat. Add the jalapeño pepper, onion and garlic and sauté for 3-4 minutes, or until the onion is softened. Add the wine, stock, tomatoes and cumin. Increase the heat to high and bring to a rapid boil, then reduce the heat to a simmer.

2. Season the fish with a little salt and pepper. If you have large chunks of fish add them now, if you have thin pieces wait until the mixture has been simmering for about 5 minutes before adding the fish. In total the fish should simmer between 8-12 minutes, or until it is cooked and flakes apart with a fork.

3. With a slotted spoon, transfer the vegetables and fish to a bowl and then add the lime juice before covering and setting aside. Raise the heat to high and allow the liquid in the pan to reduce for about 5 minutes, stirring frequently and watching carefully so that it doesn't dry up or burn. Take a few tbsp of this reduced mixture and stir it through the sour cream to give it a great flavour boost.

4. Warm the tortillas or taco shells according to the directions on the package.

5. Prepare your tacos by filling the tortillas or shells with fish, vegetables and a sprinkle of fresh cilantro. Spoon some of the sour cream mixture over top, add a little lettuce and enjoy!

Blackwood Lane Ahi Tuna

Featuring Blackwood Lane Pinot Gris

Charles Herrold, winemaker and co-owner of Blackwood Lane Winery, has shared this wonderful recipe for Ahi Tuna. Charles' time working in Hawaii exposed him to many ways of preparing this versatile fish, but this recipe is his favourite. Feel free to adjust the amount of wasabi paste according to taste. You can also add some mixed sesame seeds to the spices to achieve the effect pictured. The Blackwood Lane Pinot Gris is a wonderful match for tuna as it has plenty of rich fruit, but also enough acidity to match the strong flavours of the fish.

Serves 4

INGREDIENTS

2 tbsp paprika

1 tbsp dried oregano

1 tbsp dried thyme

1 tbsp minced garlic

1 pinch cayenne pepper

sea salt and freshly ground black
  pepper

½ cup unsalted butter

½ tsp wasabi paste

1 pinch ground cumin

¼ cup white wine

¼ cup balsamic vinegar

4 tbsp low-sodium soy sauce

1 tbsp black sesame seeds (optional)

1½ lb sashimi grade tuna loin

pickled ginger for garnish (optional)

1. In a small bowl, mix together the paprika, oregano, thyme, garlic, cayenne and salt and pepper to taste. Set aside for later use.

2. In a small saucepan over medium-high heat, mix ¼ cup of butter with the wasabi paste, cumin, wine, vinegar and soy sauce. Allow the sauce to reduce and add the sesame seeds as it starts to thicken, about 10-15 minutes.

3. Meanwhile, melt the remaining ¼ cup of butter and completely coat the tuna loin with the melted butter. Coat the tuna in the mixed spices.

4. In a large non-stick pan over high heat, sear the tuna for approximately 45-60 seconds on each side. Do not overcook; tuna is best served rare.

5. Slice the tuna loin into ¼-inch thick slices. Drizzle the sauce over the plated fish and garnish with some pickled ginger or herbs and thinly sliced vegetables.

Cherry Point's Cajun Salmon with a Barley Cream Reduction

Featuring Cherry Point Vineyards Coastal White

Chef Nick Browning has provided this favourite from Cherry Point's Bistro. Wild salmon can be found throughout the pristine coastal waters of BC and sockeye is the most sought after of the salmon species because of its firm, full-flavoured red flesh. The blackening spice used in this recipe is sometimes called Cajun spice and can be found in the spice section of the supermarket. The Coastal White at Cherry Point is a Germanic-style blend that is a great match for seafood and spice.

Serves 4

INGREDIENTS

2 tsp sea salt

1 tbsp blackening spice

4 sockeye salmon fillets (6 oz each)

2 tbsp olive oil

4 shiitake mushrooms, thinly sliced

1 garlic clove, crushed

1 cup white wine

4 cups cooked barley

1 cup whipping cream

1 red pepper, diced

3 cloves roasted garlic (pg. 32)

½ cup grated Parmesan cheese

¼ cup cooked baby shrimp

2 green onions, sliced

salt and freshly ground black pepper

1. Preheat the oven to 400°F. To prepare the salmon, scatter the salt and blackening spice on a flat surface. Place the salmon, flesh side down, on the spices to coat it. Heat a large frying pan over medium-high heat and add 1 tbsp of oil. When the oil is hot, add the salmon, flesh side down, and allow to sear for 45 seconds. Flip to the other side for 30 seconds and then transfer to a baking tray and place in the oven for 4-5 minutes. Set aside and keep warm.

2. Meanwhile, heat the remaining 1 tbsp of oil in the pan over medium-high heat and sauté the mushrooms for 1-2 minutes, until tender. Add the garlic and wine and allow the liquid to reduce by half. Stir in the barley, cream, red pepper and roasted garlic. Reduce the heat just before it boils and simmer until the liquid has reduced and reached a porridge-like consistency. Add the cheese, shrimp and onions and stir through.

3. Serve the barley mixture on a plate topped with the salmon. Add any desired vegetables on top. Serve with a glass of Cherry Point Coastal White and enjoy!

Opposite: Traditional First Nations masks hang in the barrel room at Cherry Point Vineyards

Fresh Dungeness Crab with Tarragon Garlic Butter

It may sound cliché, but it's true; the simple things in life often are the best! Here we allow the sweet, natural flavours of the Dungeness crab to shine and we simply enhance them with a wine and tarragon garlic butter. Sauvignon Blanc is crisp and delicate enough to add a delicious burst of acidity to the crab meat. So get out, set the crab traps and get that bottle chilled.

Serves 4-6

INGREDIENTS

4 live Dungeness crabs (1½ lb each)
salt
1½ cups butter
4 garlic cloves, crushed

¼ cup Sauvignon Blanc
1 tbsp lemon juice
2 tbsp chopped fresh tarragon (or 1 tbsp dried tarragon

1. Place the live crabs in the freezer for 15 minutes before cooking. This slows them down, making them easier to handle. It's also been suggested that this is a more humane way to cook them since they are in a semi-dormant state.

2. Bring a large pot of salted water to a roiling boil. Make sure there is enough water to completely submerge the crabs. Add about 1 tbsp of salt for every 4 cups of water. Add the crabs, return to a boil and cook for about 12-15 minutes, depending on the size of the crabs. Smaller crabs will cook in about 12 minutes, but bigger much bigger crabs may take up to 20.

3. Turn off the heat and remove the crabs using tongs. Run them under cool water so that they are easier to handle. To remove the shell, hold the bottom of the crab in one hand and use the thumb of your other hand to get under the top shell, prying it off and pulling it away from the body. Reserve the top shell.

4. Flip the crab over and remove the triangular section of the shell from the bottom. Flip the crab again and remove the gills (the spongy bits on the sides), the intestine down the centre of the back and the mouthparts at the front. Rinse the crab under running water and clean out any gunk from the body cavity. Rinse the top shell and then place it back on top of the crab body so it looks like a whole crab.

5. To prepare the butter, simply combine the butter and garlic in a small saucepan over medium heat. When the butter has melted completely, add the wine, lemon juice and tarragon and allow to simmer for 5 minutes.

6. Serve the crabs on a platter, with the butter in small pots for dipping. You will need some finger bowls and plenty of napkins as crab feasts can get messy. Accompany with a crisp salad, fresh bread and bottle of Sauvignon Blanc.

Oliver Twist Pinot Noir Grilled Salmon

Featuring Oliver Twist Estate Winery Pinot Noir

It doesn't get any easier than this delicious recipe provided by Oliver Twist Winery. It proves that with a few high-quality ingredients you can create a simple culinary masterpiece. Pinot Noir is fabulous served with salmon and by using it as both a marinade and a basting sauce you really make the most of this fabulous pairing.

Serves 4

INGREDIENTS

4 salmon steaks   cayenne pepper to taste
1 cup Pinot Noir   sea salt to taste

1. Place the salmon in a bowl or dish and cover with the Pinot Noir. Cover and refrigerate for 2-3 hours, turning once.

2. Remove from the fridge and transfer the salmon to a plate, reserving the wine for basting. Season the fish with cayenne pepper and salt to taste.

3. Cook the fish on a lightly greased, medium-hot grill for 6-7 minutes, turning once about halfway through. Baste with the reserved wine once, at the beginning of the cooking process. The fish is done when it flakes with a fork. Serve with your favourite salad or vegetables and a glass of Oliver Twist Pinot Noir.

Barbecued Seafood Skewers

Tasty food on a stick is always popular and these incredible seafood skewers are bound to be the hit of any barbecue. You can use any firm-fleshed fish for this recipe; tuna, halibut or even squid make wonderful substitutes or additions. The simple wine marinade can also be used for other BBQ seafoods.

Serves 4

INGREDIENTS

¼ cup olive oil

2 garlic cloves, crushed

1 tbsp chopped fresh thyme

1 tbsp chopped fresh oregano

¼ cup white wine

salt and freshly ground black pepper

8 large scallops

8 large prawns, peeled

14 oz boneless, skinless salmon fillet, cut into 1-inch cubes

1 large red pepper, cut into 1-inch pieces

1 large green pepper, cut into 1-inch pieces

1. If you are using wooden skewers, presoak them in water for at least 20 minutes so they do not burn on the grill.

2. In a large non-reactive bowl, combine the oil, garlic, herbs, wine and salt and pepper to taste. Add the seafood and peppers and mix so that they are all well coated. Cover and refrigerate for 20 minutes.

3. Thread the skewers alternating between seafood and bell pepper. Place on a preheated, lightly greased grill over medium heat. Close the lid. After about 3 minutes, baste with the marinade and then flip the skewers, close the lid and cook for another 3 minutes, or until the salmon flakes apart with a fork.

4. Serve the seafood skewers with rice and salad.

Middle Mountain Mead's Oyster Masala

Featuring Middle Mountain Mead Green Tea Elixir

Middle Mountain Mead is located on Hornby Island, which is blessed with bountiful oysters on its beaches. The owners have provided this oyster recipe, which they created using their Green Tea Elixir, one of their most popular creations. Mead is low in tannins and astringency, making it a perfect complement to spicy Asian foods!

Serves 6

INGREDIENTS

2 tbsp olive oil

1 onion, finely chopped

2-inch piece ginger root, finely grated

6 garlic cloves, minced

1 large handful fresh cilantro, finely chopped

1 tsp garam masala

1 tsp red chili powder

1 cup dry Mead (or dry white wine)

½ cup coconut cream

50 shucked medium-sized oysters

salt to taste

1. Heat 1 tbsp of oil in a frying pan over medium-high heat. Sauté the onion, ginger and 3 of the minced garlic cloves for 3-4 minutes until softened. Add the cilantro and mash everything together to make a masala paste.

2. Heat the remaining 1 tbsp of oil in a wok or large frying pan over medium-high heat and add the remaining garlic, masala paste, garam masala and chili powder. Sauté for 3-4 minutes before adding the mead and coconut cream. Just before the mixture boils, add the oysters, then reduce the heat and simmer for 15 minutes. Add salt to taste.

3. Serve over basmati rice and enjoy with a glass of Middle Mountain Mead Green Tea Elixir.

Thornhaven's Crispy Ginger Fish

Featuring Thornhaven Estates Gewürztraminer

This Asian-inspired dish uses white-fleshed fish and ginger to make an incredible fish fry up. It is the kind of dish that would normally be found at top-end Chinese restaurants. The ginger works in harmony with the spicy, crisp, clean flavours of the Thornhaven Gewürztraminer to create a wonderful match.

Serves 4

INGREDIENTS

1½ tbsp cornstarch

1 egg, beaten

1¼ lb boneless, skinless halibut or snapper fillets, cut into 2-inch pieces

2 tbsp soy sauce

2 tbsp Gewürztraminer

2 tbsp white wine vinegar

1 tbsp sesame oil

¼ cup sugar

1 cup peanut (or canola oil)

2 medium carrots, sliced diagonally

2 tbsp grated ginger

2 garlic cloves, crushed

2 green onions, sliced diagonally

1. Beat the cornstarch with the egg. Dredge the fish through the egg so that each piece is coated. Set the coated fish aside.

2. To make the sauce, combine the soy sauce, wine, vinegar, sesame oil and sugar. Mix well until the sugar dissolves. Set aside.

3. Heat the oil in a wok or large pan until very hot. Carefully place the fish in the hot oil separating the pieces and making sure they do not crowd the pan. You may need to do this in batches if the pan isn't big enough. Fry the fish until it is crispy and golden brown on each side, about 3-4 minutes per side. Transfer the cooked fish to a plate lined with paper towel to drain.

4. Carefully drain off the oil, except 1 tbsp, from the wok or pan. Return to the heat then add the carrots, ginger and garlic and fry for 1-2 minutes. Add the green onion and fry for another minute before adding the sauce mixture. Bring to a boil and stir for about 1-2 minutes before returning the fish to the pan. Mix well and remove from the heat. Serve over rice accompanied by a glass of chilled Thornhaven Gewürztraminer.

Silkscarf's Baked Fish with Pine Nuts and Raisins

Featuring Silkscarf Winery Chardonnay

This rich, colourful Mediterranean-style fish dish from Silkscarf is cooked in their fabulous, fruity Chardonnay. Not only does the dish look and taste great, but it's full of healthy goodness. Packed with lean protein, potassium and vitamins B12 and C, you can't go wrong with this one.

Serves 4

INGREDIENTS

4 halibut or bass fillets (6-7 oz each)
¼ cup lemon juice
salt and freshly ground black pepper
7 tbsp olive oil
¼ cup corn oil
4 potatoes, sliced
3 garlic cloves, crushed
3 green onions, chopped
2 tomatoes, chopped

1 lb spinach, hard stems removed and slightly chopped
¼ cup raisins
½ cup pine nuts
½ cup chopped fresh parsley
¼ tsp curry powder
1 orange, peeled and sliced
1 cup dry white wine

1. Marinate the fish in the lemon juice for 30 minutes. Season with salt and pepper.

2. Preheat the oven to 400°F. While the fish is marinating, mix 4 tbsp of olive oil and the corn oil in a large frying pan over medium heat. When the oil is hot, fry the potato slices on both sides until just softened, about 20 minutes. Transfer the slices to a baking dish and season with salt and pepper.

3. In the same pan, lightly fry the fish fillets for 2-3 minutes per side and transfer to the baking dish on top of the potatoes.

4. Add the garlic, onions and tomatoes to the pan. Sauté for 4-5 minutes and then layer them on top of the fish. Add the spinach to the frying pan and sauté for 2–3 minutes until softened. Place on top of the other vegetables.

5. Clean the pan if necessary and add the remaining 3 tbsp of olive oil. When the oil is hot, sauté the raisins and pine nuts for about 2 minutes, until the pine nuts are golden. Scatter the mix evenly on top of the spinach. Sprinkle the chopped parsley and the curry powder over top and add salt and pepper to taste. Lay the orange slices on top and then pour the wine over the entire dish.

6. Cover the baking dish with foil. Bake for 35 minutes, then remove the baking dish from the oven and drain the pan juices into a cup. Pour the juice over top of the fish, cover the dish and return to the oven for 10 minutes. Serve with a green salad or on a bed of couscous accompanied by a glass of Silkscarf Chardonnay.

River's Bend Seafood Risotto

Featuring River's Bend Winery Pinot Gris

Winery Director Gary Faessler has devised this fantastic seafood risotto recipe to be accompanied by the delicious River's Bend Pinot Gris, which is fresh, lively and pairs perfectly with the seafood in this dish. You can substitute the seafood for whatever is fresh and available in your area. The key to a good risotto is to use hot stock and to keep stirring!

Serves 6

INGREDIENTS

5 cups chicken or fish stock
2 cups water
¼ tsp saffron
4 tbsp olive oil
1 tbsp butter
1 small onion, diced
1 rib celery, diced
2 cups arborio rice (risotto rice)
2 garlic cloves, crushed

2 tbsp chopped fresh flat-leaf parsley
½ cup white wine
juice from ½ lemon
¼ tsp red chili flakes
salt and white pepper
8 large scallops, chopped
16 prawns, peeled
18 small mussels, cooked and shelled
2 cups cooked crab meat

1. Bring the stock, water and saffron to a gentle simmer in a medium-sized saucepan.

2. Heat 3 tbsp of olive oil and the butter in a large, heavy-bottomed pot over medium heat. Add the onion and celery and sauté for 2-3 minutes until tender. Add the rice, garlic and 1 tbsp of parsley and stir for 2 minutes, until the grains are well coated and translucent. Be careful not to brown the rice; turn the heat down if the pan seems too hot. Add the wine, lemon juice, chili flakes and a little salt and white pepper and stir until the wine is absorbed, about 3 minutes.

3. Add ½ cup of the simmering stock to the rice, stirring constantly, until the liquid is absorbed. Continue adding stock, about 1 cup at a time, stirring constantly. Wait until the stock has been absorbed before adding more. It should take about 15-20 minutes. The rice should be creamy and tender, but slightly firm in the middle. With the last of the stock, add the seafood, the remaining tbsp of parsley and tbsp of olive oil and mix gently. If the risotto is a little dry, just add a bit more hot stock.

4. Cover the pot and remove from the heat. Let it rest for about 5 minutes, until the scallops and prawns are cooked. Add salt and pepper to taste. Divide the risotto equally among bowls. This dish looks great garnished with parsley, dill and lemon wedges.

Quails' Gate Salt Spring Island Mussels Steamed in Chenin Blanc

Featuring Quails' Gate Chenin Blanc

Winery Chef Roger Sleiman has designed this simple, elegant dish, which is sure to impress your dinner guests. As part of the Ocean Wise™ program, Quails' Gate uses sustainable seafood in their restaurant and recipes; the mussels used to create this recipe came from Salt Spring Island. With genuine fruit sweetness to balance its firm acidity, Chenin Blanc is the quintessential seafood wine.

Serves 2-4

INGREDIENTS

3 lb live mussels

1 tbsp butter

3 shallots, sliced

2 garlic cloves, chopped

2 tomatoes cored, seeded and diced

1¼ cups Chenin Blanc (or dry white wine)

sea salt and freshly ground pepper

2 tbsp chopped fresh basil

2 tbsp chopped fresh Italian parsley

1. Discard any mussels that have damaged shells or that will not close when you tap them gently against the counter. Scrub the mussels and remove the beards by tearing them out of the shell. Rinse the mussels under clean running water.

2. Heat the butter in a large pot over medium heat. Sauté the shallots in the hot butter until translucent, about 3 minutes. Add the garlic, tomatoes, mussels, wine and salt and pepper to taste. Bring to a boil, then cover and let the mussels steam for about 5-6 minutes, or until their shells have opened. You may have to shake the pot a few times while cooking.

3. Once the shells have opened, divide them among the bowls with the sauce. Discard any mussels that did not open. Top with fresh basil and parsley and serve immediately with crusty bread and a chilled glass of Quails' Gate Chenin Blanc.

St. Hubertus Estate's Smoked Salmon and Asparagus Pasta

Featuring St. Hubertus Estate Winery Pinot Blanc

Smoked salmon and asparagus are two of the most elegant foods on the planet. This delightfully simple recipe from St. Hubertus combines both in a delicious pasta sauce unlike any other. You can use candied salmon and whipping cream for full-blown luxury and a sweeter taste, or you can substitute for smoked salmon and light cream. Either option is to die for.

Serves 4

INGREDIENTS

1 lb dried pasta

2 tbsp olive oil

1 onion, finely chopped

24 spears asparagus, cut into 2-inch pieces

½ cup Pinot Blanc

14 oz smoked salmon, chopped

2 tsp white mustard seeds

2 cups whipping cream

2 tbsp chopped fresh basil

1. Cook the pasta according to the instructions on the package.

2. Heat the oil in a large pan over medium-high heat and sauté the onion for 3-4 minutes, until transparent. Add the asparagus and sauté for 2 minutes.

3. Add the wine, salmon, mustard seeds and cream. Bring the mixture to a boil, then reduce the heat and simmer uncovered for approximately 10-15 minutes, until slightly thickened. Stir in the chopped basil. Serve the pasta topped with the sauce and enjoy with a chilled glass of St. Hubertus Pinot Blanc.

Vintage memories St. Hubertus Estate Winery

Thai-Style Green Curry Salmon

This wonderful Thai curry can also be made with chicken or other seafoods. Just alter the cooking time to make sure the meat is cooked the way you like it. Try and avoid the light coconut milk as it does not give the same rich and creamy texture. You can find Thai curry paste and fish sauce in the Asian section of the supermarket. Feel free to experiment with red or yellow curry pastes as well; they all have wonderful flavours and work equally well.

Serves 4

INGREDIENTS

1 can coconut milk (14 oz)

1 tbsp green Thai curry paste

3 tbsp fish sauce

1 tbsp sugar

⅓ cup white wine

1½ lb boneless, skinless salmon, cut into 1-inch cubes

½ cup chopped fresh cilantro

1. Mix the coconut milk, curry paste, fish sauce, sugar and wine in a medium-sized saucepan over medium heat. Stir until all of the curry paste is mixed into the cream sauce.

2. Add the salmon and ¼ cup of cilantro and simmer for 10-15 minutes, or until the salmon is just cooked and flakes apart with a fork. Don't overcook the salmon!

3. Serve immediately with rice or pasta and top with the remaining ¼ cup of fresh cilantro.

Diane's Rich Seafood Fettucini

This seafood fettucini is very rich, but oh so good! Combining fresh BC seafood with cream, cheese, wine, garlic and mushrooms, it's easy to make and it will impress even the most discerning guests. Sadly, the creator of this recipe, Diane, is no longer with us, but you can raise a glass to her memory as you enjoy this incredible dish!

Serves 8-10

INGREDIENTS

½ cup butter
1 medium onion, finely chopped
2 large garlic cloves, minced
2 cups sliced fresh mushrooms
1½ tsp dried basil
1 tbsp garlic powder
1 tsp sugar

salt and freshly ground black pepper
4 cups whipping cream
1 cup grated Parmesan cheese
10 oz each shrimp, scallops, crab
⅓ cup white wine
1½ lb fresh fettucini

1. Heat the butter in a large, deep pan over medium heat. Sauté the onions and garlic until tender, about 4-5 minutes. Add the mushrooms, basil, garlic powder, sugar and salt and pepper to taste and continue to cook for another 10 minutes.

2. Add the whipping cream and ½ cup of Parmesan cheese. Increase the heat and bring almost to a boil, then quickly reduce the heat and simmer for 10 minutes. Add the seafood and wine, simmer for about 30 minutes to thicken the sauce and blend the flavours.

3. Meanwhile, cook the fettucini according to the directions on the package.

4. Transfer the cooked pasta to a large pasta bowl and cover with the sauce and the remaining ½ cup of cheese. Toss well to coat, then cover and let stand for 15 minutes. Serve with garlic bread and plenty of chilled wine.

Red Rooster's Tuna and Black Olive Farfalle

Featuring Red Rooster Pinot Blanc

This recipe from Red Rooster Winery takes the classic tuna pasta and turns it into a gourmet feast. The slow-cooked garlic gives the sauce its deep flavour. For the very best results, use good quality olives and tuna that has been canned in oil. Farfalle pasta is sometimes sold as "bow-tie pasta". The Red Rooster Pinot Blanc is elegant and light enough to let the Mediterranean flavours of this dish shine through, but it still has enough concentrated fruit and weight to hold its own without getting lost.

Serves 4

INGREDIENTS

¼ cup olive oil

8 large garlic cloves, halved

¼ tsp cumin seeds

3 tbsp chopped fresh parsley

¾ lb dried farfalle

3 anchovy fillets, rinsed and chopped

1 cup pitted black olives, chopped

½ cup white wine

½ tsp fennel seeds, crushed

1 pinch red pepper flakes

1 can tuna, drained (6 oz)

1 tbsp capers

1 tbsp grated lemon zest

salt and freshly ground black pepper

1. Heat the olive oil in a large pan over medium-low heat. Add the garlic, cumin seeds and 2 tbsp of parsley. Cook for about 20 minutes, or until the garlic is tender. Don't allow the garlic to brown or it will become bitter.

2. Meanwhile cook the farfalle according to the directions on the package. Reserve ½ cup of the pasta water, then drain and set the pasta aside in a covered pot to keep warm.

3. Add the anchovy fillets, olives, wine, fennel seeds, reserved pasta water and red pepper flakes to the garlic mixture. Stir well and cook for 1 minute before removing from the heat.

4. Stir in the tuna, capers, remaining tbsp of parsley and lemon zest. Add salt and pepper to taste. Divide the hot pasta among individual pasta bowls and top with the sauce. Enjoy with a chilled glass of Red Rooster Pinot Blanc.

Poultry

Eat, drink and be merry for tomorrow we may diet.

Harry Kurnitz 1908 – 1968

Herb and Wine Roasted Chicken with Gravy

Everyone has a favourite recipe for roast chicken and this is ours. The wine and stock combined in the pan keeps the bird moist while roasting and makes a juice that turns into a fabulous garlic-infused gravy. Once you've tried a bird cooked in wine, you won't look back!

Serves 6

INGREDIENTS

1 tbsp dried oregano

1 tbsp dried basil

1 tbsp dried thyme

1 tbsp paprika

½ cup butter

1 large chicken (5-6 lb)

1 large onion, quartered

5 garlic cloves, halved

1 cup chicken stock

1 cup white wine

salt and freshly ground black pepper

1. Preheat the oven to 375°F. In a small bowl, combine the dried herbs and paprika with the butter. Pat the chicken dry with a paper towel, then carefully lift the chicken skin and rub the herb butter between the skin and the breast. Get as far in as possible without damaging the skin. Rub the butter all over the outside of the skin as well. Season the cavity of the chicken with salt and pepper, then insert the onion quarters into the cavity. Using a skewer or string truss the legs together.

2. Put the chicken into a roasting pan (on a small rack if you have one) with the garlic cloves and pour the wine and chicken stock directly over the bird. Bake in the oven, basting with pan juices every 20-30 minutes, until a meat thermometer inserted into the thickest part of the thigh reads 180°F. This should take about 2 hours for a 5-6 lb bird, but always check the internal temperature so that you don't under or overcook the chicken.

3. Remove the chicken from the pan and tent loosely with foil. Let the bird rest for about 30 minutes before carving. Using a spoon or fork, mash up the cooked garlic cloves into the pan juices and stir well to make the gravy. This method is much more flavourful than gravy thickened with flour. Reheat the gravy just before serving.

Avocado Tex-Mex Chicken

This delicious creation was inspired by some of the many Mexican grape pickers, who head north looking for seasonal work during harvest time. As many as 2,000 workers cross the border each year to participate in BC's Seasonal Agriculture Worker Program. Wine and Mexican food make a great combination; it's best if you look for a white with a touch of spice to balance any heat in the food. As usual, feel free to adjust the heat on this one to suit your own personal taste.

Serves 4

INGREDIENTS

4 boneless, skinless chicken breasts

salt and freshly ground black pepper

4 tbsp all-purpose flour

2 tbsp olive oil

1 tbsp butter

1 small onion, chopped

1 garlic clove, crushed

6 button mushrooms, sliced

¼ cup chicken stock

¼ cup white wine

1 small avocado, mashed

1 cup grated cheddar cheese

3 tbsp chopped canned jalapeños

1. Preheat the oven to 350°F. Cover the chicken breasts with plastic wrap or wax paper. Using the flat side of a meat mallet or a rolling pin, gently pound the breasts and flatten them out to about ½-inch thick. Season them with a little salt and pepper and dredge them in 3 tbsp of flour.

2. Heat the oil in a large pan over medium-high heat and then add the chicken breasts. Cook for about 5 minutes on each side or until they are golden brown and almost cooked through. Transfer the chicken to a baking dish and set aside.

3. Add the butter to the pan and when it is hot, add the onion, garlic and mushrooms. Sauté for 2-3 minutes and then add the remaining 1 tbsp of flour. Stir through and then add the chicken stock and wine. Simmer for 5-6 minutes, stirring frequently, until slightly thickened. Add the mashed avocado and ¼ cup of the grated cheese and stir through until it is well mixed.

4. Spread the sauce over top of the chicken in the baking dish. Top with the remaining ¾ cup of grated cheese and sprinkle with the chopped jalapeño peppers. Bake for 10-15 minutes or until the cheese is melted and the chicken is cooked through.

5. Serve with Mexican-style rice, fried potatoes or any of your favourite Tex-Mex side dishes.

Cranberry Turkey Burgers

This recipe takes all of the traditional elements of a turkey dinner and turns them into a delicious burger. You get the flavours of the turkey, the stuffing, the cranberry sauce and the wine in each and every bite. They work equally well fried in a pan or grilled on the BBQ. You may like to melt some Havarti cheese on top for the final few minutes of cooking and for an added taste sensation, try a little cooked bacon on top.

Serves 5

INGREDIENTS

½ onion, finely diced

½ tbsp poultry seasoning

½ tsp salt

1 lb ground turkey

1 egg, beaten

¼ cup dried cranberries

½ cup breadcrumbs

¼ cup white wine

freshly ground black pepper

5 burger buns

your favourite burger toppings

1. In a large bowl, mix together the onion, poultry seasoning, salt, turkey, egg, cranberries, breadcrumbs, wine and a little black pepper. With wet hands, form the mixture into 5 patties. Place the patties in the fridge to rest for 15-30 minutes; this will help them to stay together while cooking.

2. Cook the burgers on a hot, lightly greased grill for about 6 minutes on each side. Only flip them once and take great care not to break them apart. Alternatively, the burgers can be cooked on a stove in a frying pan with a little oil. In this case start cooking at medium-high and then reduce the temperature to medium after one side has browned. Make sure that the burgers are cooked through.

3. Serve the burgers on fresh buns with your favourite toppings. We enjoy our turkey burgers topped with Dijon mustard, mayonnaise, Havarti cheese and red onion.

Summerhill's Burned Lavender Chicken with Cherry Croissant Pudding

Featuring Summerhill Pinot Noir

Summerhill Chef Jesse Croy shares this incredible lavender chicken recipe that is perfect for summer when the lavender is in bloom. The exquisite Summerhill Pinot Noir is combined with cherries in the croissant pudding portion of this dish. Pinot Noir pairs exceptionally with fowl, especially with these chicken thighs, grilled with burned lavender and fresh summer herbs.

Serves 4-5

INGREDIENTS

10 boneless chicken thighs

1 tsp + a pinch sea salt

3 tbsp dried or fresh lavender

3 juniper berries (optional)

3 tbsp grapeseed oil (or light olive oil)

1½ cups pitted cherries

1 cup Pinot Noir

5 roughly cracked peppercorns

2 shallots, chopped

5 large day-old croissants, cubed

2 eggs

1¾ cups whipping cream

1 pinch nutmeg

1 tbsp chopped fresh thyme

1 tbsp chopped fresh summer savory

1. Rinse and dry the chicken thighs, then rub them with 1 tsp of salt, lavender, juniper berries and oil. Place them in the fridge to marinate while the pudding is being prepared.

2. Preheat the oven to 350°F. Combine the cherries, wine, peppercorns and shallots in a medium-sized saucepan over medium-high heat. Bring to a boil and then simmer until the wine is reduced by half. Strain, reserving both the liquids and the solids.

3. Place the croissants in a large mixing bowl with the reserved cherries and shallots. In a separate bowl, beat the eggs and 1 cup of cream with the nutmeg and a pinch of sea salt. Add the cream mixture to the croissant mixture and stir through. Pack the mixture into a bread or loaf pan, then cover with foil and bake for 20 minutes. Remove from the oven and allow to set for 10 minutes.

4. Meanwhile, to make the sauce, combine the remaining ¾ cup of cream, reserved wine, thyme and savory in a small saucepan over medium-high heat. Bring to a boil and then simmer until the mixture has reduced by half. Set aside.

5. While the sauce is reducing, cook the chicken on a lightly greased grill over medium-high heat for about 8 minutes per side, with the lid closed, until the chicken is thoroughly cooked and the juices run clear when pricked.

6. To serve, turn the pudding pan upside down, remove the pudding and divide it among the individual plates. Place the grilled thighs on top of the pudding and drizzle with the sauce. Serve with grilled summer squash or seasonal vegetables.

Tantalus Alsace-Style Roast Chicken in Riesling

Featuring Tantalus Old Vines Riesling

This traditional recipe from Tantalus Vineyards was adapted from a recipe found in Bon Appetit magazine. The recipe's origins lie in the Alsace region of France, where dry Rieslings are the norm. At Tantalus, Riesling is taken very seriously and this tasty dish allows the wine to shine, while providing an assortment of delicious and unusual flavours for you to enjoy.

Serves 4

INGREDIENTS

½ cup olive oil

8 shallots, peeled and chopped

4 carrots, peeled and chopped

5 ribs celery, roughly chopped

2 heads garlic, cloves separated and peeled

salt and freshly ground black pepper

1 whole chicken (4 lb)

4 sprigs rosemary

4 sprigs thyme

20 pitted prunes

½ small green cabbage, cut into wedges

½ cup low-sodium chicken broth

1 cup Riesling

1. Preheat the oven to 450°F. Heat 2 tbsp of oil in a large frying pan over medium-high heat. Add the shallots, carrots, celery, garlic cloves and salt and pepper to taste. Sauté until the vegetables are lightly browned, about 8 minutes, then transfer them to a large baking dish or casserole and push to the sides to make room for the chicken.

2. Heat 2 tbsp of oil in the same pan over medium-high heat. Season the chicken generously with salt and pepper. Add the chicken to the pan and brown it on all sides; this usually takes about 10 minutes. Transfer the chicken, breast side up, to the baking dish in the centre of the vegetables. Arrange the rosemary, thyme, prunes and cabbage around the chicken with some cabbage stuffed underneath.

3. Pour off any fat from the frying pan. Add the chicken broth and wine to the pan and bring to boil scraping up any browned bits from the bottom of the pan. Pour the hot mixture over and around the chicken. Pour the remaining ¼ cup of oil over top. Cover the baking dish or casserole with foil and seal it on the sides. If you have a lid, place this on top as well. Roast for about 70 minutes, until a meat thermometer inserted into the thickest part of the thigh reads 180°F. Let the chicken rest, covered loosely in the foil, for 10-15 minutes before serving.

4. Serve the chicken on a platter, breast side up, surrounded by vegetables. Season the pan juices to taste with salt and pepper and then pour them over the chicken. Carve and enjoy!

Wine-Braised Chicken Thighs with Tarragon and Leek

The use of tarragon in this dish results in a classic French-style feast. Tarragon has a wonderful aroma and flavour that is hard to beat. As with all French cooking, wine makes a great addition to the sauce and the table. You could also use boneless, skinless chicken thighs or breasts in this recipe. Just reduce the simmering time of the chicken by about half.

Serves 4

INGREDIENTS

8 chicken thighs

salt and freshly ground black pepper

2 tbsp olive oil

3 tbsp butter

1 large leek, finely chopped

1 cup white wine

½ cup chicken stock

2 tbsp chopped fresh tarragon

1 tsp lemon juice

1. Season the chicken with salt and pepper. Heat the oil in a large pan over medium-high heat. Add the chicken and brown for about 4 minutes on each side. Remove the chicken from the pan and set aside. Drain off any excess fat from the pan and return it to the heat.

2. Lower the heat to medium, melt 2 tbsp of butter and then add the leek. Sauté for about 6-7 minutes, then add the wine, chicken stock and tarragon and bring to a boil. Reduce the heat to a simmer and return the chicken to the pan. Cover and simmer for about 25-30 minutes until the chicken is cooked through.

3. Remove the chicken from the pan and raise the heat to high, stirring constantly. After 2-3 minutes, add the lemon juice and remaining 1 tbsp of butter and stir through. Remove from the heat and add salt and pepper to taste.

4. Serve the chicken with the leek sauce and accompany with scalloped potatoes and a chilled glass of white wine. Bon appétit!

Wok-Fried Pinot Noir Chinese Chicken

If you love going out for Chinese food, but never get it quite right when you try it at home, then this dish is for you. It is very quick and easy and the results are fantastic. Traditionally a dish like this would use rice wine, but we prefer to use Pinot Noir. If you don't have Pinot Noir, then you can substitute for another light red wine; Gamay Noir or even Rosé would be good choices.

Serves 4

INGREDIENTS

4 tbsp cornstarch

1 egg, beaten

salt and freshly ground black pepper

1 lb boneless, skinless chicken breast
  or thighs, cut into 1-inch pieces

3 cups peanut or canola oil

4 small chili peppers, chopped
  (optional)

6 green onions, chopped

2 tbsp soy sauce

1 garlic clove, crushed

2 tbsp fish sauce

2 tsp sugar

1 tbsp grated ginger

2 tbsp Pinot Noir

1. In a large bowl, combine 2 tbsp of cornstarch with the egg and a little salt and pepper. Add the chicken and stir to coat with the mixture. Sprinkle the remaining 2 tbsp of cornstarch over top of the coated chicken pieces.

2. Heat the oil in a wok over high heat for about a minute before lowering the heat a little. The oil should be at 350°F for cooking. To test the temperature, drop a small piece of bread into the oil and it should brown in about 15 seconds.

3. Using tongs, transfer the chicken pieces to the hot oil to cook for about 2 minutes, or until golden brown and crisp on the outside. Using tongs or a slotted spoon, transfer them to a plate lined with paper towel. You may need to do a few batches.

4. When all of the chicken is cooked, remove the wok from the heat and carefully drain off most of the oil, leaving about 2 tbsp. Return the wok to the heat and add the chilies and green onions. Fry for about 1 minute before transferring them to the chicken plate.

5. Add the soy sauce, garlic, fish sauce, sugar, ginger and wine to the wok and stir well for about 2-3 minutes, allowing the sauce to thicken slightly. Return the chicken and onions to the pan and allow to cook for another 2 minutes, stirring well.

Calona's Boneless Chicken Breasts Simmered in Wine and Cream

Featuring Calona Vineyards Sovereign Opal

Every now and again, we come across a recipe that tastes so much better than the sum of all its parts; this is one of those recipes. The flavour produced by combining these simple ingredients is incredible. Sovereign Opal, which was invented in BC and is only produced by Calona, is perfect for this dish with its rich, lusciousness and a hint of spice. For those who are watching their calories, you can substitute the whipping cream for light cream.

Serves 4

INGREDIENTS

2 tsp chili powder (or to taste)	4 tbsp butter
1½ tsp onion powder	2 garlic cloves, minced
salt and freshly ground black pepper	¼ cup white wine
4 boneless, skinless chicken breasts	½ cup whipping cream

1. Combine the chili powder, onion powder and a little salt and pepper in a small bowl then rub the seasonings into the chicken breasts.

2. In a large pan over medium heat, melt 2 tbsp of butter. Add the chicken breasts to the pan and cook on one side for about 3 minutes. Flip the breasts, add the garlic and sauté for another 3-4 minutes. Add the wine and allow to cook for another 2-3 minutes.

3. Add the cream and stir well. Just before the cream boils, reduce the heat to a simmer and allow the sauce to thicken; this may take 3-4 minutes. Add the remaining 2 tbsp of butter and stir through. Once the butter is completely melted and incorporated into the sauce, remove from the heat.

4. Transfer the chicken breasts to individual plates, pour the sauce over top and serve immediately with mashed potatoes and steamed vegetables

Stoneboat's Duck Breast with a Blackberry Pomegranate Reduction

Featuring Stoneboat Vineyards Pinotage

This recipe was created by the proprietors of Stoneboat Vineyards for a family Pinotage tasting. Pinotage is a rich wine with red berry flavours and it makes a lovely reduction that is perfect for duck. The tartness of the pomegranates and the fragrance of the blackberries really complete the sauce. Duck is best served medium-rare; if you cook it too long the flavour will really change.

Serves 4

INGREDIENTS

1½ cups red wine
1½ cups pomegranate juice
2 shallots, chopped
1 garlic clove, minced
5 black peppercorns
1½ cups duck or chicken stock
½ cup water

½ cup sugar
1½ cups blackberries
1 tbsp lemon zest
2 tbsp butter
4 duck breasts
salt and freshly ground black pepper

1. Combine the wine, pomegranate juice, shallots, garlic and peppercorns in a large saucepan over medium heat. Bring to a boil and then simmer until the liquid has reduced by about ⅓. Strain through a fine sieve and discard the solids. Add the stock and reduce again until you have 1½-2 cups of liquid.

2. Meanwhile, in a small saucepan, combine the water and sugar and bring to a boil over medium-high heat. Add the blackberries and lemon zest and allow to simmer for 3-4 minutes. Do not cook any longer or the berries will disintegrate.

3. Whisk the butter into the wine reduction from step 1. Using a slotted spoon, add the cooked blackberries and gently stir through. You can also add some of the sugar-water from the blackberry pan if additional sweetness in the sauce is desired. Set aside.

4. Season the duck breasts well with salt and pepper. With a sharp knife, score the fat in a crisscross pattern, taking care not to pierce through to the meat. Heat a non-stick pan over medium-low heat, then add the duck breasts, fat side down. Allow the fat to render for about 6-8 minutes.

5. Once most of the fat has rendered, drain some of it off (this is great for sautéing cabbage or potatoes) and turn up the heat to medium-high for a few minutes, allowing the skin to brown and crisp. Flip the breasts and cook for a further 2-3 minutes, or as needed to bring to medium-rare. The breast should be springy to touch.

6. Slice the breasts crosswise into 4 or 5 pieces and serve on a plate with the sauce drizzled over top. Accompany with mashed potatoes, green vegetables and a glass

Crispy Roasted Cornish Game Hens with Winter Vegetables

Cornish game hens look and taste impressive and they are quite simple to prepare and roast. This dish, created by River's Bend's in-house culinary expert Gary Faessler, is roasted with Chardonnay in the pan. When combined with the herbs, butter and pan drippings, it creates a delicious sauce to serve over top of the hens. As an option you may like to stuff the hens with a classic bread and herb stuffing. To be safe and avoid risk of contamination, be sure that the stuffing is cooled and the birds are stuffed just prior to roasting.

Serves 6

INGREDIENTS

6 Cornish game hens (1 lb each)
salt and freshly ground black pepper
3 tbsp unsalted butter
12 small carrots
6 large shallots

3 small turnips, halved
6 red potatoes, halved
2 bay leaves
6 sprigs thyme
1½ cups Chardonnay

1. Position the oven rack in the center of the oven and preheat to 400°F. Rinse the hens inside and out with cold running water and pat dry with paper towels. Tuck the wing tips under the hens and season the whole birds with salt and pepper. If stuffing is desired, pack it into the hens and tie the legs together to hold its shape. Place the hens breast side up in a large shallow roasting pan.

2. Rub each of the hens with ½ tbsp of butter. Add all of the remaining ingredients to the pan. Roast the hens until they are cooked through and juices run clear when the thigh is pierced, about 45 minutes. A meat thermometer inserted into the deepest part of the thigh should read 165°F.

3. Remove from the oven and transfer the hens to a serving platter. Loosely tent with foil and let rest for 10 minutes. To serve, place 1 hen on each plate, divide the caramelized vegetables among the plates and spoon the pan juices over the hens.

Bread and Herb Stuffing

This simple recipe complements the meal and still allows the flavours of the bird to be the star. Melt ½ cup of butter in a saucepan and add 3 crushed garlic cloves, 2 cups of chopped celery and 1 cup of chopped onion. Sauté until tender, then transfer to a bowl. Add 1 lb of dried bread cubes, 1 tbsp of seasoning salt, 1 tbsp of poultry seasoning, ½ cup of chopped parsley, 2 tbsp of fresh chopped sage and 2 cups of chicken stock. Stir so that the bread is moist. Allow the mixture to cool completely before loosely stuffing the birds. Do not overstuff!

Walnut and Parmesan Crusted Chicken Breasts with Chardonnay Butter

Parmesan chicken is an old classic, but here we make it even tastier by adding a delicious crust of toasted walnuts and a Chardonnay butter. This is a simple dish that can be prepared in minutes, but its gourmet flavours will make you seem like a culinary genius. Walnuts are delicious and healthy and now you can even find a walnut wine at Vista D'oro Winery in Langley.

Serves 4

INGREDIENTS

4 boneless, skinless chicken breasts
salt and freshly ground black pepper
½ cup breadcrumbs
½ cup grated Parmesan cheese
⅓ cup walnuts, crushed

2 tbsp all-purpose flour
1 egg, beaten
2 tbsp olive oil
2 tbsp butter
¼ cup Chardonnay

1. Season the chicken with salt and black pepper. In a large bowl, combine the breadcrumbs, cheese and crushed walnuts. Dredge the chicken breasts in flour, then dip the breasts into the beaten egg and thoroughly coat with the walnut crumbing mixture.

2. In a large pan over medium heat, combine the oil and 1 tbsp of butter. When the butter is hot and beginning to bubble, add the crumbed chicken breasts. Cook for about 7 minutes per side, or until each side is golden brown. Remove the chicken from the pan and add the wine. Using a spatula or wooden spoon, scrape up any browned bits from the bottom of the pan.

3. Allow the wine to reduce by half, about 3 minutes, then add the remaining 1 tbsp of butter. Once the butter has melted, drizzle the Chardonnay butter sauce over top of the cooked chicken breasts. Serve with mashed potatoes and asparagus.

Turkey Sausage Skewers with a Dijon, Honey and Red Wine Drizzle

This recipe is easy on the budget and it's full of wonderful flavour. It will prove popular with adults and children alike. You are not limited to turkey sausages; beef or pork sausages also work very well. The sausages should be precooked on the grill first so that they slide onto the metal skewers easily. You can also experiment by adding different vegetables; cherry tomatoes, cubed eggplant pieces and button mushrooms all make excellent additions.

Serves 4

INGREDIENTS

1½ tbsp Dijon mustard

1½ tbsp honey

3 tbsp red wine

3 tbsp olive oil

1 garlic clove, crushed

3 tbsp balsamic vinegar

¼ tsp salt

2 red peppers, cut into 1-inch pieces

1 red onion, cut into 1-inch pieces

8 turkey sausages, cooked and cut into
 3 equal pieces

1. If you're using wooden or bamboo skewers, presoak them in water for about 20 minutes so they don't burn on the grill.

2. In a large bowl, whisk together the mustard, honey, wine, oil, garlic, vinegar and salt. Add the red peppers and onion, mixing well to ensure that the vegetables are well coated. Allow the vegetables to marinate for 15 minutes to infuse the flavours.

3. Thread the skewers, alternating between a piece of sausage, red pepper and onion.

4. Place the skewers on a grill over medium-high heat. Keep an eye on them and turn occasionally so that they do not burn. You can baste them while they cook with the leftover marinade, but save some to drizzle over top when they are done. They will take about 10 minutes on the grill and they are ready when the vegetables are starting to soften.

5. Once plated, drizzle the remaining sauce over top of the skewers and serve immediately with rice.

Meat

Water for oxen. Wine for kings.

Old Spanish proverb

Morning Bay's Tagliatelle with Traditional Bolognese Sauce

Featuring Morning Bay Estate Bianco

This traditional bolognese recipe comes from Barbara Reid at Morning Bay Winery. The sauce can also be used for lasagne by placing it in alternating layers with béchamel sauce, lasagne noodles and mozzarella. The sauce is thick and flavoursome and a white wine with plenty of acidity, like the Bianco, holds up nicely to this dish. For a more modern version of the sauce you can add some chopped garlic in with the onions and celery. For the best results, leave time for a long simmer.

Serves 4

INGREDIENTS

3 tbsp olive oil

5 tbsp butter

1 cup finely chopped onion

1 small carrot, diced

1 rib celery, diced

1 lb lean ground beef

salt and freshly ground black pepper

¾ cup white wine

½ cup whole milk

1 pinch ground nutmeg

1 can chopped tomatoes (14 oz)

1 lb dried tagliatelle

½ cup grated Parmesan cheese

1. Heat the olive oil and 3 tbsp of butter in a heavy, deep saucepan over medium-high heat. Add the onion and sauté for about 3-4 minutes, until slightly softened. Add the carrot and celery and continue sautéing for about 2-3 minutes.

2. Add the beef, breaking it up with a wooden spoon. Add some salt and pepper and continue to cook, stirring occasionally, until the meat is just browned. Add the wine and simmer until it has completely evaporated. Add the milk and nutmeg, stirring until most of the milk has evaporated. Stir in the tomatoes and once they start to bubble, turn the heat down very low. Simmer uncovered for at least 3 hours, stirring occasionally. Season with salt and pepper if necessary.

3. Cook the pasta according to the instructions on the package. Drain and toss with the remaining 2 tbsp of butter and the freshly grated cheese. Add the sauce, toss again and serve at once.

8ᵗʰ Generation Back Bacon and Veggie Casserole

Featuring 8ᵗʰ Generation Chardonnay

This recipe from winery owner Stefanie Schales is perfect for chilly fall and winter evenings. Stefanie often prepares this dish during the fall crush for her husband (and winemaker) Bernd. The dish is full of wonderful vegetables such as Kohlrabi, a type of German turnip. This recipe combines traditional German cooking with a bottle of BC wine and the results are spectacular. As Stefanie says, "How can life get any better?"

Serves 6-8

INGREDIENTS

1 tbsp vegetable oil
2½ lb Canadian back bacon, sliced
1 small onion, finely chopped
1 garlic clove, chopped
1 carrot, chopped
1 kohlrabi, chopped (optional)
1 leek, chopped
1 small purple-topped turnip, chopped

1 small parsnip, chopped
1 rib celery, chopped
½ tbsp vegetable stock powder
1 cup Chardonnay
6 small mushrooms, halved
1 small apple, peeled, cored and cut
    into 8 pieces
1¾ cups whipping cream

1. Preheat the oven to 350°F. Heat the vegetable oil in a stoveproof casserole dish over medium-high heat. Sauté the bacon for 2-3 minutes, until lightly browned, then remove the bacon from the casserole and set it aside. You may need to do this in batches.

2. Add the onion, garlic, carrot, kohlrabi, leek, turnip, parsnip and celery to the casserole and sauté for 5 minutes. Add the stock powder, wine, mushrooms and apple. Bring to a boil, then reduce the heat and simmer until all of the liquid has evaporated.

3. Return the bacon to the casserole and layer it between the vegetables. Pour the cream over top and bake it in the oven until the top has lightly browned, about 30-40 minutes. Season with a little salt and pepper to taste.

4. This dish is delicious served with corkscrew pasta and a glass of 8ᵗʰ Generation Chardonnay.

Lamb Shank Osso Bucco

This is another incredible recipe from River's Bend Winery's culinary genius Gary Faessler. In this superb rainy autumn dish, the lamb becomes meltingly soft, juicy and fall-off-the-bone tender after it slow cooks in aromatic braising liquids. If the dish is prepared in advance, the flavour will deepen and mellow. The gremolata is a traditional garnish that imparts a fresh citrus note to brighten this rich and meaty dish.

Serves 6

INGREDIENTS

3 tbsp finely chopped flat-leaf parsley

1 tsp grated lemon zest

5 garlic cloves, 1 minced and
  4 chopped

3 tbsp olive oil

1 tbsp butter

6 lamb shanks

salt and freshly ground black pepper

1 cup all-purpose flour

1 medium onion, diced

1 rib celery, diced

1 carrot, finely diced

2 bay leaves

2 tbsp chopped fresh herbs (thyme,
  oregano or sage)

2 cups red wine

2 cups chicken stock

1 can diced tomatoes (14 oz)

1. Make the gremolata by mixing together the parsley, lemon zest and minced garlic clove in a small bowl. Set aside.

2. Add the olive oil and butter to a large heavy-bottomed pan over medium-high heat. Season the lamb shanks with salt and pepper. Dredge the shanks in the flour, coating each side completely, then tap off any excess. Sear the shanks until brown on all sides, about 8 minutes. Do not crowd the pan; brown 2 or 3 shanks at a time if necessary. Remove the shanks and set aside.

3. Reduce the heat to medium. Add the onion, celery and carrot to the pan and sauté for 3 minutes. Stir in the chopped garlic cloves, bay leaves, and herbs and sauté for 1 minute. Deglaze the pan with the red wine, scraping the bottom and sides to loosen the browned bits. Add the stock and tomatoes. Bring the liquid to a boil and then reduce the heat to a simmer.

4. Place the shanks back into the pan, making sure they are immersed at least halfway; if not add more stock. Cover the pan and braise the shanks over medium-low heat, basting and turning the shanks occasionally, until the sauce is stew-like and the meat is very tender, about 1½-2 hours.

5. Remove the bay leaves, sprinkle the gremolata over the lamb shanks and serve immediately with risotto, creamy polenta or mashed potatoes.

Gray Monk's Seared Venison Short Loin with a Blueberry-Merlot Reduction

Featuring Gray Monk Estate Odyssey Merlot

Gray Monk Estate Winery Chef Willi Franz created this wine-country recipe using venison from the Nicola Valley and blueberries from the Okanagan. The dish also includes some delicious potato galettes. Since venison is such a lean meat it's best served medium rare; if you cook the meat too long it will become dry. This dish is divine served with the robust Gray Monk Odyssey Merlot, which has the deep fruit and structure to hold its own alongside flavourful meat dishes and strong cheeses.

Serves 4

INGREDIENTS

3 tbsp grapeseed oil (or light olive oil)
2 tbsp finely chopped onions
1 tsp crushed black peppercorns
1 cup Merlot
1 tbsp balsamic vinegar
1 cup veal or beef stock
1 tbsp butter
1 tbsp sugar
⅔ cup blueberries

6 medium potatoes, peeled and cut
    into ½-inch cubes
1 egg yolk
2 tbsp cornstarch
2 tbsp breadcrumbs
1 pinch nutmeg
salt and freshly ground black pepper
1 venison short loin, trimmed (1½ lb)
½ cup crumbled blue cheese

1. Heat 1 tbsp of oil in a saucepan over medium-high heat and sauté the onions for 2-3 minutes, until golden brown. Add the crushed peppercorns, wine, vinegar and stock and allow the liquid to reduce by ⅔.

2. In a separate saucepan, melt the butter and sugar over medium heat. Add the blueberries and cook for 2-3 minutes. Add the wine reduction to the blueberry mix and simmer for five more minutes. Set aside.

3. To make the potato galettes, boil the potatoes in lightly salted water until soft. Mash them and allow to cool. Mix the potatoes with the egg yolk, cornstarch, bread crumbs, nutmeg and salt and pepper to taste. Form the mixture into 4 large patties and set aside.

4. Heat 1 tbsp of oil in a pan over medium-high heat, sear the venison for about 7 minutes on each side. Pay close attention to the meat; do not overcook it. Let the meat rest for 10 minutes before slicing.

5. While the meat is resting, heat the remaining tbsp of oil in a frying pan over medium heat and fry the galettes until they turn golden brown. At the same time, gently reheat the blueberry-Merlot reduction.

6. To serve, drizzle the blueberry-Merlot sauce over the sliced venison, then top with the crumbled blue cheese just before serving. Accompany with the potato galettes, your favourite veggies and a glass of Gray Monk Merlot.

Peller Estates Merlot and Cocoa Marinated Beef Kaisers

Featuring Peller Estates Merlot

Executive Chef Jason Parsons of Peller Estates has shared this fabulous recipe that combines cocoa and Merlot to create a mouth-watering marinade for beef. Served on a Kaiser with cheese and Dijon mustard, this dish adds a fine-dining touch to any barbecue. Pink peppercorns are actually dried berries and they are commonly available in supermarkets, but you can substitute for green peppercorns or even black if you can't find them.

Serves 4

INGREDIENTS

4 strip loin steaks (4 oz each)

2 cups Merlot

3 garlic cloves, chopped

3 sprigs rosemary

2 tbsp cocoa powder

1 tbsp pink peppercorns

1 stick cinnamon

salt and freshly ground black pepper

4 slices aged cheddar

4 kaiser buns

4 tsp Dijon mustard (or to taste)

1. Place the steaks in a large resealable plastic bag. Add the wine, garlic, rosemary, cocoa, peppercorns and cinnamon. Seal the bag and leave it to marinate in the fridge for a minimum of 1 hour.

2. Remove the steaks from the marinade and season with salt and pepper. Grill on a hot barbecue for about 3-4 minutes per side for medium, or until the meat reaches the desired doneness. Melt the cheddar on the steaks for the last minute of grilling; this works best with the lid down.

3. Lightly toast the kaisers on the grill while the meat is cooking, taking care not to burn them. Spread them with the Dijon mustard, place the steaks on top and serve immediately.

Granite Creek Estate Pork Chops with Port Wine Sauce

Featuring Granite Creek Merlot Fortified Wine (Port Style)

This recipe from Granite Creek Estate Winery turns a pork chop into a fabulous gourmet treat. If necessary, you can substitute the wine jelly for regular fruit jelly. We've tested this recipe with red current jelly and the results were fantastic. The port-styled wine used in the sauce gives it a deep, rich flavour and it's a wonderful accompaniment for the pork.

Serves 4

INGREDIENTS

2 tbsp butter

4 thick-cut pork chops

3 shallots, chopped

1 garlic clove, chopped

⅓ cup Port wine jelly (or red wine jelly)

1½ tbsp Dijon mustard

1 cup port-style wine

1 tsp cornstarch mixed with 1 tbsp water

salt and freshly ground black pepper

1. Melt the butter in a frying pan over medium heat. Add the pork chops and brown them for 4-5 minutes on each side, until they are just cooked through. Remove the chops from the heat, but cover them to keep warm.

2. Add the shallots and garlic to the pan and stir until soft and golden, about 3 minutes. Add the wine jelly and Dijon mustard, stirring until well blended.

3. Raise the heat to medium-high, slowly stir in the port-style wine and cook until the mixture has reduced by about ⅓.

4. Stir in the cornstarch-water mixture and simmer, stirring occasionally, for 1–2 minutes. Add salt and pepper to the sauce as desired.

5. Spoon the sauce directly over the pork chops and serve immediately accompanied by your favourite vegetables.

Wine Jelly

Wine jelly is becoming more and more popular and it is easy to make. However, if you don't want to make your own, they make great wine jellies at Granite Creek Winery and another fabulous BC producer is Lone Willow (www.winejelly.ca).

To make your own wine jelly, bring 2 cups of wine to a boil in a small saucepan over high heat, reduce the heat to a simmer and stir in 3 cups of sugar. When it's well combined, stir in a pouch of liquid pectin and stir for 1 minute further. Pour the mixture into hot sterilized jars, filling them about ¼ inch from the rim. Seal, while everything is still hot, with sterilized new lids. To get more creative and add complexity to the flavours, you can add herbs like thyme and basil, or even a little red wine vinegar.

Nk'Mip Cellars Pepper-Crusted Beef Tenderloin Steaks

Featuring Nk'Mip Cellars Qwam Qwmt Pinot Noir

Chef Charles Stover at Nk'Mip (in-ka-meep) came up with this recipe using ostrich before he tried it with beef and he says the results are equally delicious. Premade demi-glace is available at supermarkets, but you can also use 1 cup of regular beef stock reduced to ½ cup over high heat, as the wine gives the sauce plenty of flavour.

Serves 4

INGREDIENTS

2 tbsp butter

4 tenderloin steaks (4-5 oz each)

2 tbsp crushed peppercorns

½ cup red wine

4 shallots, diced

½ cup demi-glace

¼ cup whipping cream

salt and freshly ground black pepper

1. Rub ¼ tbsp of butter into each steak, then coat the steaks with the crushed peppercorns. Melt the remaining tbsp of butter in a skillet over medium-high heat. Add the steaks and cook for about 3-5 minutes on each side for medium-rare, or until the meat reaches the desired doneness. Transfer the cooked steaks to a plate and cover loosely with foil.

2. Deglaze the pan by adding the wine, shallots and demi-glace. With a wooden spoon scrape up any browned bits from the bottom of the pan. Bring to a rapid boil and allow the liquid to reduce by at least half. Add the cream, stir through and simmer for an additional minute. Season to taste with salt and additional black pepper if desired. Plate the steaks, top with the sauce and serve with roasted potatoes and vegetables.

A statue depicting a First Nations rider welcomes visitors to Nk'Mip Cellars

Wellbrook's Barbecued Leg of Lamb
with a Balsamic Fruit Glaze

Featuring Wellbrook Blueberry Wine

This recipe was created by Glenys Morgan, a guest chef at the "Wining and Dining at Wellbrook Winery" cooking school series. Glenys uses blueberry wine to give a fruity burst to the succulent lamb meat, but other fruit wines give equally delicious results. When purchasing the leg of lamb ask for it to be butterflied by the butcher. If you don't have a BBQ, you can roast the lamb in the centre of a 400°F oven for 20-25 minutes, or until a meat thermometer reads 125°F for rare. Make sure you plan this one in advance as the meat requires 24 hours to marinate.

Serves 6

INGREDIENTS

1½ cups sun-dried fruit (eg. cherries, figs, prunes, etc.)

½ cup + 2 tbsp brown sugar

½ cup demi-glace (or 1 cup beef stock reduced over high heat to ½ cup)

2 cups fruit wine

1 cup balsamic vinegar

3 sprigs fresh rosemary

3 sprigs fresh sage

4 garlic cloves, crushed

¾ cup olive oil

1 leg of lamb, butterflied (3 lb)

salt and freshly ground black pepper

1. Combine the fruit, ½ cup of brown sugar, demi-glace, 1 cup of fruit wine and ½ cup of balsamic vinegar in a saucepan over medium-high heat and bring to a boil. Reduce the heat and simmer for 6-7 minutes. Taste the sauce and add a touch more sugar or demi-glace if desired. If the sauce is too acidic, stir in a tbsp of cold unsalted butter. Allow the sauce to cool, then transfer to the fridge until needed.

2. In a large resealable plastic bag, combine the rosemary, sage, garlic, ¼ cup of olive oil and the remaining 1 cup of wine. Add the lamb, flattening out the meat, then seal and refrigerate for 24 hours. Turn several times during the marinating process to distribute the liquid.

3. Remove the meat from the marinade and pat dry. In a separate bowl, combine remaining ½ cup of olive oil, ½ cup of vinegar and 2 tbsp of brown sugar. Coat the meat with the mixture and season with salt and pepper.

4. For charcoal grills, pile the charcoals to one side; for gas grills, preheat one side to high and leave the other turned off. Sear the roast over high heat, turning frequently to develop a good crust. It should take about 3-4 minutes per side, but watch for burning. Move the seared lamb to the indirect heat, opposite the charcoals or away from the gas flame area and close the lid. Turn the meat frequently, or as needed. For rare meat, cook until a meat thermometer registers 125°F. A 3 lb butterflied roast should take about 20 minutes to cook. Transfer the meat to a platter, tent loosely with foil and let it rest for 15 minutes before carving.

5. While the lamb is resting, reheat the sauce on low. To serve, cut the lamb thinly across the grain and spoon the sauce over the lamb slices. Serve with roasted potatoes.

Golden Beaver Winery's Danish Frikadeller

Featuring Golden Beaver Pinot Noir Dry Rosé

This traditional Danish dish with a twist is a family favourite of winery owners Stella Schmidt and Bruno Kelle. The frikadeller is a tasty cousin of the Swedish meatball. The wine not only adds flavour, but also keeps them light and airy. You can always freeze any leftovers if there are any.

Serves 4-6

INGREDIENTS

2 lb lean ground pork

1 large onion, finely chopped

2 eggs

1 tsp salt

2 garlic cloves, crushed

1 tsp freshly ground black pepper

¾ cup all-purpose flour

1¼ cups Rosé

3 tbsp olive oil

1. In a large bowl, mix together the pork, onion, eggs, salt, garlic, pepper and flour. Stir in the wine a little at a time; the mixture should be light and airy. Let it rest about 20 minutes in the fridge.

2. Shape the frikadeller by heaping a tablespoon, covered in warm oil, with meat and pressing it against the inside of the bowl, forming oval-shaped patties 3-4 inches long.

3. Heat the oil in a large pan over high heat. Brown the frikadeller on both sides, for about 2-3 minutes, then reduce the heat to medium-low and fry for about 10-15 minutes, turning occasionally. Serve piping hot with traditional Danish fare, such as boiled potatoes and creamed peas and carrots. Top with gravy or the pan drippings and enjoy with a glass of Golden Beaver Rosé.

Twisted Tree's Seared Pepper Steaks in a Creamy Merlot Sauce

Featuring Twisted Tree Merlot

This delicious recipe using the luscious Twisted Tree Merlot combines all sorts of fabulous flavours to create a sauce that will have your guests begging for the recipe. This dish is easily adaptable for lamb chops, veal, game meats or even chicken.

Serves 4

INGREDIENTS

4 New York steaks (8 oz each)

1 tbsp sea salt

2 tbsp freshly ground black pepper

1 tbsp olive oil

1 large shallot, chopped

1 cup Merlot

3 tbsp oyster sauce

1 tbsp soy sauce

1 tbsp Dijon mustard

½ cup whipping cream

1 tbsp chilled butter

1. Preheat the oven to 400°F. Season each steak on both sides with sea salt and ground pepper. Heat the oil in a large pan over high heat. Add the steaks and sear for about 2 minutes on each side.

2. Transfer the steaks to a baking tray and place in the oven for about 5 minutes for medium rare. When cooked to the desired doneness, remove the steaks from the oven, tent loosely with foil and allow them to rest. Reserve any pan juices.

3. While the steak is in the oven, reduce the heat on the stovetop to medium-high. Add the shallot to the pan and sauté for about 1 minute until slightly softened. Add the wine and scrape up any browned bits with a wooden spoon. Bring to boil and allow the wine to reduce to ⅓, about 7-9 minutes.

4. Add the oyster sauce, soy sauce, mustard, whipping cream and steak juices from the baking tray and bring to a boil, stirring constantly, until the sauce is slightly thickened. Reduce the heat to low and add the butter, mixing through until melted.

5. Serve the steaks topped with the incredible sauce, accompanied by mashed potatoes, green beans and a glass of Twisted Tree Merlot.

Burrowing Owl Braised Short Ribs

Featuring Burrowing Owl Estate Winery Merlot

Burrowing Owl Winery Chef Bernard Casavant shares with us this delicious and easy-to-prepare recipe for short ribs. This dish tastes even better the next day, although, we'd be surprised if you have any leftovers. The succulent meat falls off the bone and your guests will be in foodie heaven if you serve this with the soft polenta recipe below and a glass of Burrowing Owl Merlot!

Serves 6-8

INGREDIENTS

3 lb beef short ribs (bone in)

1 tbsp sea salt

freshly ground black pepper

2 tbsp canola oil

1½ cups diced onion

1 large carrot, peeled and diced

¾ cup chopped celery

2 garlic cloves, crushed

1 large tomato, diced

1 sprig fresh rosemary (or 4 tbsp dried)

3 sprigs fresh thyme (or 2 tbsp dried)

1 cup Merlot

6 cups beef stock

1. Preheat the oven to 350°F. Season the ribs with salt and pepper. Heat the oil in a roasting pan, or Dutch oven over medium-high heat and then sear the short ribs for about 5 minutes per side, or until they turn a deep-brown colour.

2. Remove the ribs from pan and set them aside. Add the onion, carrot, celery, garlic, tomato and herbs and sauté for 4-5 minutes. Add the wine and allow it to reduce by ¾, about 10-12 minutes.

3. Place the short ribs back in the roasting pan and add the beef stock. Bring to a simmer, cover with a lid or tinfoil and place the pan in the oven for 1½ hours, until the short ribs are fork tender.

4. Remove the pan from the oven and carefully transfer the short ribs to a platter, cover lightly with foil to keep warm. Skim off any fat from the top of the liquid, then strain and discard the solids. Return the liquid to the pan and bring to a boil over high heat. Allow it to reduce by ⅔, so that you only have 2 cups remaining. Taste the liquid and add salt and pepper if desired. Pour the sauce over the plated meat and accompany with soft polenta or mashed potatoes.

Soft Polenta

In a large saucepan over medium-high heat, melt 1 tbsp of butter. Sauté 2 tbsp of minced shallots and 1 tsp of minced garlic for a few minutes until browned. Deglaze the pan with 2 tbsp of white wine, then add 4 cups of vegetable or chicken stock, ¾ cup of whipping cream, 1 tbsp salt and a pinch of black pepper. Bring to a simmer, then whisk in ¾ cup of cornmeal. Simmer until the cornmeal is no longer gritty, about 40 minutes. Stir through ½ cup of grated Parmesan cheese. Serve immediately.

Italian Sausage and Tuscan Bean Casserole

This easy-to-prepare casserole is perfect for warding off those weeknight winter blues. It is quick to make and very suitable for those nights when you don't want to spend a lot of time in the kitchen. You can also change the flavour dramatically by trying out different types of sausages and/or beans. Red wines like Syrah, Merlot, Cabernet Franc or Cabernet Sauvignon would all be great with this dish, or you can stick with the Italian theme and use a BC Barbera.

Serves 4-6

INGREDIENTS

1 tbsp olive oil
10 Italian-style sausages
1 onion, chopped
4 ribs celery, chopped
1 red pepper, chopped
2 tbsp tomato paste

1 tbsp all-purpose flour
1 cup red wine
2 cups chicken stock
1 can white beans, drained and rinsed
  (19 oz)

1. Heat the oil in a large pan over medium heat. Add the sausages and cook until they are browned all over, about 5-6 minutes. Remove them from the pan and set them aside.

2. Add the onion, celery and red pepper to the pan and cook for 5 minutes, stirring occasionally. Add the tomato paste and flour and stir through until it is well combined. Add the red wine and chicken stock. Bring to a boil and allow about ⅓ of the liquid to evaporate before reducing the heat to a simmer.

3. Slice the sausages diagonally into thick slices, then add them to the simmering mixture. Continue to simmer for about 15 minutes, stirring occasionally, before adding the beans. Keep cooking for another 5-6 minutes until the beans are warmed through.

4. Serve with mashed potatoes or rice and accompany with a glass of red wine.

Opposite: A summer view of Okanagan Lake

Meat

Road 13 Goat Cheese Stuffed-Pork Loin with Fennel and a Pinot Reduction

Featuring Road 13 Pinot Noir

Korrine Bremner, resident food and wine expert at Road 13, has devised this wonderful recipe for pork loin stuffed with creamy, tangy goat cheese. You can make this dish year-round using cherries that are fresh, frozen or canned and if you want to try something a little different, you can use blueberries instead. The flavours of the dark fruit in the Pinot Noir are enhanced by the fruit in the Pinot reduction and the soft tannins make it a perfect match for pork.

Serves 4

INGREDIENTS

1 pork tenderloin (about 1 lb)

salt and freshly ground black pepper

6 oz soft goat cheese

lemon zest from ½ lemon

¼ cup olive oil

1 small fennel bulb, thinly sliced

2 cups Pinot Noir

1 cup pitted cherries, sliced

2 tbsp blackberry jelly

1 tbsp balsamic vinegar

1. Preheat the oven to 350°F. Slice the pork loin lengthways, but not all the way through. Cover with plastic wrap and use a meat tenderizer or rolling pin to pound it out to an even thickness of around ½ inch. Season the meat with salt and pepper.

2. In a small bowl, mix together the goat cheese, lemon zest and pepper to taste. Lay the cheese mixture along the centre of the loin then roll it up and tie with some string to secure.

3. Rub the meat with the olive oil and then brown all sides in a large pan over medium-high heat. Transfer the meat to a baking dish and bake for 20-30 minutes, or until the meat is fully cooked.

4. Using the pan that the meat was browned in, sauté the fennel for 2 minutes. Add 2 tbsp of wine to deglaze the pan. Using a wooden spoon or spatula, scrape up any browned bits from the bottom of the pan.

5. Pour in the remaining wine and bring to a boil. Reduce the heat and simmer for 15 minutes allowing the wine to reduce. Add the cherries, jelly and vinegar and allow to simmer for another 4-5 minutes. The liquid should be reduced to about 1 cup.

6. When the pork loin is ready, remove it from the oven and allow it to rest for 5 minutes before slicing. Spoon the sauce over top of the meat and serve immediately.

Salt Spring Vineyards Tender Moroccan Lamb Tagine

Featuring Salt Spring Estate Vineyards Pinot Noir

Salt Spring Vineyard's Colleen Bowen is well known for her incredible wine-country cooking. This recipe is no exception and the exotic flavours in the dish combine beautifully with the earthy, fruitiness of the Pinot Noir. Salt Spring Island is famous for it's organic free-range lamb. When buying a leg of lamb, ask for it to be deboned. Give yourself enough time to marinate the meat for 6 hours and cook it for 3 hours when you are preparing this recipe. The results are well worth the wait.

Serves 4

INGREDIENTS

1 lemon, juiced, zest reserved
10 garlic cloves, crushed
½ cup sun-dried tomatoes
2 tbsp olive oil
¼ tsp crushed chili peppers
½ tsp ground cinnamon
1 pinch saffron
½ tsp cumin seeds
salt and freshly ground black pepper
1 deboned leg of lamb, sliced thickly

4 medium potatoes, sliced
2 yams, chopped
½ lb green beans
1 cup chopped green and black olives
1 cup mixed dried apricots and figs
1 cup Pinot Noir
1 lemon, quartered
1 tbsp cornstarch mixed in 2 tbsp
   warm water (optional)

1. Preheat the oven to 325°F. In a large non-metallic bowl or resealable plastic bag, combine the lemon juice and zest, garlic, sun-dried tomatoes, olive oil, crushed chili peppers, cinnamon, saffron, cumin and salt and pepper to taste. Add the meat and cover it thoroughly in the marinade, refrigerate and allow to soak for at least 6 hours, turning occasionally.

2. In this sequence, layer the following in a tagine or a large casserole with a lid: potatoes, yams, sliced meat, beans, olives, dried fruit, marinade, Pinot Noir and the quartered lemon.

3. Cover and cook for 3 hours. If you find the sauce is too runny, you can thicken it in a saucepan on the stovetop. Stir the cornstarch mixture into the sauce and allow the sauce to simmer for a few minutes to thicken. This dish is fantastic served over couscous, but it's also delightful on its own. Serve with a glass of Salt Spring Pinot Noir for a taste of perfection.

Poplar Grove's Beef Short Ribs with Stone Fruit Relish and Blue Cheese

Featuring Poplar Grove "The Legacy"

This recipe was created by Chef Roger Planiden who is renowned throughout BC for his fabulous wine-inspired creations. You will need to plan ahead for this recipe as it takes 4 hours to marinate the meat and 4 hours to bake it, but the results are definitely worth the time. The succulent wine-infused meat falls off the bone and the rich, contrasting flavours of the blue cheese and fruit create an elegant dish that pairs wonderfully with a complex, blended red wine such as "The Legacy".

Serves 6

INGREDIENTS

2 cups red wine

¼ cup chopped fresh thyme

¼ cup chopped fresh rosemary

2 bay leaves

¼ cup black peppercorns

6 boneless beef short rib medallions
 (about 8 oz each)

salt and freshly ground black pepper

2 tbsp olive oil

1 cup + 1 tbsp diced shallots

2 garlic cloves

1 tbsp tomato paste

1 tbsp butter

1½ tbsp water

1½ tbsp raspberry vinegar

2½ tsp sugar

2 fresh nectarines, diced (or 1 cup
 dried apricots, diced)

6 slices blue cheese (2 oz each)

1. In a large dish, combine the wine, thyme, rosemary, bay leaves and peppercorns. Add the meat, cover and refrigerate for 4-6 hours, turning occasionally.

2. Preheat the oven to 285°F. Remove the meat from the marinade and season with salt and black pepper. Reserve the marinade. In a large hot pan over medium-high heat, sear the meat until golden brown on all sides, about 3 minutes per side. Transfer the meat from the pan to a casserole dish.

3. Return the pan to the heat and add the olive oil. Sauté 1 cup of diced shallots and garlic for about 2 minutes. Add the tomato paste and allow it to caramelize for a couple of minutes. Add the marinating liquid and simmer for 1 minute, using a wooden spoon to scrape up any browned bits from the bottom of the pan. Pour the liquid over the short ribs in the casserole. Cover and bake for 4 hours.

4. Remove the meat from the casserole, transfer it to a plate and cover loosely with foil to keep warm. Skim off the fat from the top of the casserole liquid, then strain the liquid into a saucepan. Reduce the liquid to a sauce consistency over high heat and then whisk in the butter.

5. To make the relish, heat the water, vinegar and sugar in a small saucepan over medium-high heat for a few minutes, until syrupy. Stir in 1 tbsp of diced shallots and the nectarines. Cook for a couple of minutes, until the fruit is soft and glazed.

6. Plate the short ribs with potatoes and roasted vegetables. Place a piece of blue cheese on top of the meat and serve with the fruit relish and red wine sauce.

Pentâge's Gourmet Meatloaf with a Caramelized Red Wine Glaze

Featuring Pentâge Winery Pentâge

This is a meaty meatloaf; it does not use breadcrumbs to fill it out like most recipes do. The Pentâge red wine glaze not only adds great flavour, but as it caramelizes, it also seals in moisture to ensure that this dish is not at all dry. By using a premium red wine, such as the delicious and complex Pentâge, with a simple gourmet dish, it allows the flavours in the wine to shine through and get the attention they deserve. The glaze for this dish can also be used as a fabulous BBQ sauce.

Serves 4

INGREDIENTS

1½ lb lean ground beef
2 garlic cloves, crushed
1 small onion, diced
1 egg
1 package onion soup mix (1½ oz)
1 tbsp olive oil

1 cup red wine
2 tbsp soy sauce
1 tbsp Worcestershire sauce
2 tbsp brown sugar
½ cup ketchup

1. Preheat the oven to 350°F. In a large mixing bowl, use clean hands to combine the beef, 1 clove of crushed garlic, ½ of the onion, egg, and soup mix together in a mixing bowl. Ensure that the ingredients are well combined. Transfer the meat mixture to a lightly greased loaf pan and bake for 35 minutes.

2. While the meatloaf is cooking prepare the glaze. Heat the oil in a small saucepan over medium heat. Add the remaining ½ of the diced onion and sauté for 4-5 minutes, or until just soft. Add the remaining crushed garlic clove and continue to cook for 1 more minute. Add the wine and allow the mixture to reduce for around 20 minutes, or until you have about ¼ cup of liquid remaining. Add soy sauce, Worcestershire sauce, sugar and ketchup and reduce the heat to low. Stir and allow to cook for 5-10 minutes, until the meatloaf is ready to come out of the oven.

3. Cover the meatloaf with the glaze and return to the oven for another 15 minutes or until cooked through. Cut the meatloaf into slices of desired thickness and serve with scalloped or mashed potatoes and steamed vegetables.

Vegetarian &
Side Dishes

My grandmother is over eighty and still doesn't need glasses.
Drinks right out of the bottle.

Henny Youngman 1906-1988

Vegetable Tempura

Tempura veggies are an awesome meal or side dish and this light crispy batter can also be used on your favourite seafoods. Tempura has been popular in Japan since the 16th century. The veggies suggested here are as a guide only and you can easily substitute these for any that you happen to have handy. Sparkling wine is the perfect accompaniment to these tasty treats as the bubbles are able to cut through the oil to refresh the palate.

Serves 4 as a side dish

INGREDIENTS

1 cup all-purpose flour

2 tbsp cornstarch

½ tsp salt

1 cup chilled sparkling wine

1 egg, beaten

3 cups vegetable oil

12 snap peas

8 asparagus spears, woody ends removed and cut into pieces

1 red pepper, cut into 2-inch strips

1 cup broccoli florets

8 button mushrooms, halved

sea salt to taste

soy sauce for dipping

1. Mix the flour, cornstarch and salt in a medium-sized mixing bowl. In a separate bowl combine the sparkling wine and egg, stirring briefly. Add the wine mix to the flour and whisk together gently until it is incorporated and you have a mixture that resembles pancake batter.

2. In a wok or deep pan, heat the oil over medium-high heat. You will know the oil has reached the right temperature when a small piece of bread sizzles when dropped into the oil. Do not put the vegetables into the oil until it reaches this point.

3. Ensure all of the vegetables are dry to avoid spattering oil, then coat the veggies in the batter. Using a slotted spoon or tongs, lower them into the hot oil, a few pieces at a time. Do not overcrowd the pan. It will only take a minute or 2 for the batter to turn a crispy golden brown. Once they are cooked, transfer the vegetables to paper towel to drain.

4. Sprinkle with sea salt to taste and serve immediately with some soy sauce for dipping. For a full meal you can serve the tempura on a bowl of rice or noodles; this is traditional Japanese fast food!

Gourmet Mac and Three Cheese

This healthier version of mac 'n' cheese will be a hit with children and adults alike. This is real macaroni and cheese; it is about as far from Kraft dinner as is possible and you don't need to serve this one with ketchup. It uses three delicious cheeses to give it depth and complexity. You could also experiment with different cheeses; pepper jack gives it a nice kick. Easy to prepare and a pleasure to eat, mac 'n' cheese remains one of the great North American comfort foods. To make it even healthier you could substitute for whole wheat macaroni.

Serves 4

INGREDIENTS

¾ lb elbow macaroni

1 tbsp olive oil

1 small onion, diced

3 garlic cloves, crushed

1 can chopped tomatoes (28 oz)

¾ cup red wine

3 tbsp chopped fresh basil

1½ tsp sugar

2 cups grated aged cheddar

2 cups grated jack cheese

½ cup grated Parmesan cheese

1. Preheat the oven to 350°F. Cook the pasta in plenty of salted water according to the instructions on the package. Drain, cover and set aside.

2. Meanwhile, heat the oil in a large pan over medium heat. Add the onion and sauté for about 4 minutes. Add the garlic and sauté for another minute.

3. Add the tomatoes and increase the heat to high. Cook, stirring frequently, for about 10 minutes until the liquid has evaporated. Reduce the heat to medium-high, then add the wine, basil and sugar. Cook for about 5-10 minutes until the liquid is nearly gone.

4. Remove the pan from the heat, mix the sauce together with the cooked macaroni, 1 cup of grated cheddar cheese and 1 cup of grated jack cheese. Transfer the macaroni mixture to a greased ovenproof dish. Cover with the remaining cheddar and jack cheese and top with the Parmesan. Bake for about 30 minutes, until the cheese is golden brown and bubbly on top. Serve immediately with garlic bread and a side salad.

Cheesy Scalloped Potatoes in Wine

Scalloped potatoes are always a hit, but add cheese and wine and you'll never go back to the original version. This recipe serves 8 as a side dish but if your friends are anything like ours, they will definitely want second helpings of this fabulous spud feast.

Serves 8 as a side dish

INGREDIENTS

1 large onion, chopped
2 cups sour cream
½ cup dry white wine
1¼ tsp salt

8-10 medium potatoes, peeled and
    sliced ¼-inch thick
2½ cups grated aged cheddar cheese

1. Preheat the oven to 350°F. Mix together the onion, sour cream, wine and salt in a large bowl. Add the potatoes to the mixture and stir through.

2. Transfer the potato mixture to a greased 9x13-inch pan. Cover with cheese and bake for 75 minutes, until the potatoes are soft and the cheese is golden on top. Let stand for 5-10 minutes before serving.

Township 7's Porcini Risotto

Featuring Township 7 Gewürztraminer

Mushroom risotto is a perfect fall dish and Township 7 Winery has come up with this simple yet impressive recipe using their spicy Gewürztraminer, which adds a fresh liveliness to the dish. Dried porcini mushrooms are available year-round and the water used to rehydrate them makes a flavourful addition to this recipe. During the fall you can always substitute them for some of BC's fresh wild mushrooms. Just fry them in a little butter before adding to the risotto.

Serves 4

INGREDIENTS

1 oz dried porcini mushrooms
1 cup boiling hot water
3 tbsp olive oil
1 shallot, diced
1½ cups arborio rice (risotto rice)
¼ cup butter

½ cup white wine
1 small bunch parsley, finely chopped
salt and freshly ground black pepper
2 cups hot vegetable stock
½ cup whipping cream (optional)
1 cup grated Parmesan cheese

1. Steep the porcini mushrooms in the boiling water for 20 minutes, then dice. Reserve the mushroom water for later use.

2. Heat the olive oil in a pan over medium-high heat. Sauté the shallot for 1-2 minutes and then add the rice and butter. Keep stirring until the rice is well coated with the oil and butter and starts to looks transparent, about 3-4 minutes. Make sure to keep stirring or the rice will burn.

3. Turn the temperature down to medium-low. Stir in the wine until it has all been absorbed into the rice, about 4-5 minutes. Add the parsley and a little salt and pepper and turn the heat down to low.

4. Start adding the stock, about 1 cup at a time, stirring constantly. When the first cup of stock has been absorbed, add the second cup. Once the second cup has been absorbed, add the reserved mushroom water (or an extra cup of stock if using fresh mushrooms). Add the cream, if desired, and stir through. The rice is done when it is creamy and tender but still has a slightly firm centre. If necessary you can add a little more stock to achieve this.

5. Finally, stir through the cheese and add salt and pepper to taste. Serve immediately.

Sonoran Estate Sushi Orani

Featuring Sonoran Estate Late Harvest Oraniensteiner

Winemaker Adrian Smits and his wife Sarah created this delicious vegetarian sushi recipe which substitutes the traditional rice wine vinegar for their exquisite late harvest Oraniensteiner. Making these rolls is easy, but you will need a bamboo sushi mat, available at most major supermarkets. You can alter the recipe by adding red pepper, cucumber, or anything else you desire. Cooked crab mixed up with some low-calorie plain yoghurt is a favourite for non-vegetarians.

Makes 5 rolls

INGREDIENTS

2 cups sushi rice

2½ cups water

pinch of salt

½ cup late harvest wine

5 pieces nori (seaweed sheets)

1 carrot, sliced into thin strips

1 ripe avocado, chopped into small pieces

small handful of snow peas, sliced thinly lengthwise

soy sauce for dipping

small amount wasabi paste

1. Prepare the sushi rice according to the instructions on the package. This usually involves the following steps: Combine the rice with water in a saucepan. Add a pinch of sea salt and heat to a boil, stirring often. When the water starts boiling, cover and reduce the heat to low, stirring occasionally. The rice will be ready in about 20 minutes from the time you first put it on the stove. Be careful not to burn it.

2. Remove the prepared rice from the heat, add the wine and stir through.

3. Place the nori sheet lengthwise on the bamboo mat, shiny side down. With wet hands, lay out ⅓-½ cup of the prepared sushi rice. Flatten so that it evenly covers the entire bottom ⅔ of the nori, leaving exposed nori at the end away from you.

4. Divide the filling ingredients into 5 even portions. Place one portion of the filling on the rice so that it runs horizontally across the centre.

5. Use the bamboo rolling mat to roll the sushi fairly tight. The ingredients form the centre of the roll. Dampened fingers will prevent sticking. Apply a little water to the nori at the far end of the roll and seal it closed. Once you have rolled the sushi, use the mat and gently squeeze the roll together so that it does not unravel when you let go. Repeat the process with the rest of the ingredients, making 5 rolls.

6. For the best results serve immediately, by cutting into 6-8 pieces with a sharp wet knife. If you are preparing in advance, wrap the roll in cling film and store in the fridge for no more than 48 hours, then cut accordingly before serving. Serve with soy sauce and wasabi paste for dipping.

Drunken Pad Thai with Cashews

Well it isn't really drunken, but adding a little wine to this recipe sure makes it a lot more fun and tasty. Most Pad Thai recipes use fish sauce, but in this vegetarian version we get a flavour boost directly from the wine. The addition of cashews is a great way to class up this traditional, but popular, peasant dish that is usually made with peanuts. Thai rice noodles are usually found in the Asian section of the supermarket.

Serves 4

INGREDIENTS

1 package Thai rice noodles (8 oz)
1 tbsp peanut oil
4 garlic cloves, crushed
1 red pepper, chopped
2 tomatoes, chopped
1 handful of snow peas, trimmed
6 oz extra-firm tofu, drained and cut
   into ½-inch cubes

¼ cup dry white wine
2 eggs, beaten
¼ cup soy sauce
2 tbsp chopped fresh cilantro
¼ cup cashews, chopped
4 green onions, chopped
½ cup bean sprouts
1 lime cut into wedges

1. Soften the noodles according to the directions on the package. This usually involves either soaking them in hot water for up to 45 minutes or submersing them in boiling water for 3-4 minutes. Drain, cover and set aside.

2. Heat the peanut oil in a wok or large pan over medium heat. Add the garlic and red pepper and stir fry for 3-4 minutes, until the pepper starts to soften. Add the chopped tomatoes, snow peas, tofu and wine and continue to fry for 4 minutes. Using a spatula push everything to one side of the wok and add the eggs. Allow them to almost completely set before breaking them apart with the spatula and mixing them through. Add the soy sauce, noodles and cilantro, stirring until everything is heated through.

3. Divide the noodles evenly among the serving plates and sprinkle the cashews and green onions over top. Garnish with the bean sprouts and a wedge of lime and serve with a chilled glass of white wine.

Wild Mushroom and Garlic Pita Pizza with a Rustic Tomato Sauce

This is an easy gourmet meal that can be thrown together in minutes using the fresh mushrooms that BC is famous for. Even if you are not into foraging yourself, most supermarkets carry a great selection of mushrooms and the earthy flavours of these wild treats are perfect for pairing with an earthy wine like Pinot Noir. The secret to a good pizza is the sauce. The rustic tomato sauce used here is full of deep, rich flavours that will turn you off the canned stuff for life.

Makes 4 individual pizzas

INGREDIENTS

4 tbsp olive oil
½ onion, diced
5 garlic cloves, crushed
1 can chopped tomatoes (28 oz)
½ cup red wine
1 tsp sugar
1 tsp salt

1 tbsp dried Italian herbs
1 lb mixed mushrooms, roughly chopped
4 pita breads
2-3 cups grated mozzarella cheese
chopped fresh parsley, chives or tarragon for garnish

1. Preheat the oven to 350°F. To make the sauce heat 2 tbsp of the olive oil in a large pan over medium heat. Add the onion and sauté for about 5 minutes. Add 2 of the crushed garlic cloves and sauté for an additional minute. Add the tomatoes with their juice and increase the heat to high. Cook for about 5 minutes, stirring frequently. Add the wine, sugar, salt and Italian herbs, then reduce the heat to medium-high. Cook for about 10 minutes, stirring occasionally, until most of the liquid has evaporated and a thick sauce remains. Remove from the heat. For a smoother sauce, you can blend the mixture in a food processor.

2. While the sauce is reducing, heat the remaining 2 tbsp of olive oil in a pan over medium heat, add the mushrooms and remaining 3 cloves of crushed garlic and sauté for 3-4 minutes, until the mushrooms have softened. Remove from the heat and set aside.

3. Place the pitas on a large, lightly greased baking tray. Spread the tomato sauce over the pitas and top with the sautéed mushrooms. Sprinkle the cheese over top and bake for about 5 minutes, or until the cheese has melted. Be careful not to burn the base or allow it to become too crispy. To brown the top of the pizzas, place the tray under the broiler for 1 minute. Sprinkle with fresh herbs to garnish. Allow the cheese to cool slightly before serving.

Stag's Hollow Spring Asparagus and Goat Cheese Risotto

Featuring Stag's Hollow Sauvignon Blanc

This delightful recipe, from winery owner Linda Pruegger was adapted from one that she found in Chatelaine. It uses fresh spring asparagus and goat cheese to create a creamy rich risotto with zing. The distinct flavours and acidity of the Sauvignon Blanc make it a wonderful partner for this dish. This risotto makes an excellent main course, or it can also be served as a side dish with salmon or lamb. If asparagus is not in season, then spinach makes a great alternative. Just add it with the goat cheese and stir through, giving it enough time to wilt.

Serves 4

INGREDIENTS

2 small bunches asparagus
1 tbsp butter
2 garlic cloves, minced
1½ cups arborio rice (risotto rice)
1 cup Sauvignon Blanc

½ tsp hot chili flakes
3 cups vegetable stock
1 cup water
¾ cup soft goat cheese
4 green onions, sliced

1. Break the woody ends off the asparagus and discard. Diagonally slice the asparagus into ½-inch pieces and set aside.

2. Melt the butter in a large saucepan over medium heat. When the butter is hot, add the garlic and sauté for about 1 minute. Add the rice and stir for 2-3 minutes, until all of the grains are coated with the butter and turning translucent. Add the wine and chili flakes and continue stirring until all of the wine has been absorbed.

3. Start adding the stock and water, about ⅓ cup at a time, stirring constantly. Wait until the stock has been absorbed before adding more. With the last of the liquid add the asparagus and continue to stir until the rice is creamy and tender, but slightly firm in the middle, and the asparagus is just cooked. The whole process should take 20-25 minutes. The mixture should still be a little soupy. If it is too dry, add a little more stock or water.

4. Stir in the goat cheese and green onions until well blended. Serve in wide, heated bowls with a chilled glass of Stag's Hollow Sauvignon Blanc.

Orofino's Harvest Spaghetti Marinara

Featuring Orofino Pinot Noir

This dish is prepared a lot around harvest time at Orofino because it is easy to prepare while sharing a conversation and a bottle of wine. It is also the perfect time for taking advantage of the gorgeous organic tomatoes that are grown in the Similkameen Valley. The complex Orofino Pinot Noir is a fabulous accompaniment to this simple dish and the rest of the bottle won't last long. This is healthy, delicious comfort food that will satisfy your hunger and leave you feeling great.

Serves 6-8

INGREDIENTS

¼ cup olive oil

1 large onion, diced

2 large ribs celery, diced

2 large carrots, diced

5 garlic cloves, crushed

2 tsp capers (optional)

10-15 medium tomatoes, diced

1 cup red wine

1 heaped tbsp sugar

salt and freshly ground black pepper

¼ cup chopped fresh basil

1½ lb spaghetti

grated Parmesan cheese to top

flat-leaf parsley for garnish (optional)

1. Heat the olive oil in a large saucepan over medium heat. Add the onion, celery and carrots and sauté for 3-4 minutes, or until the onion is soft and translucent. Stir in the garlic, capers and tomatoes.

2. After about 20 minutes, when the tomatoes have broken down and started to bubble, stir in the wine. Add the sugar along with salt and pepper to taste. Finally stir in the basil leaves.

3. Transfer the sauce to a blender or food processor and blend in batches. Return the sauce to the pan and simmer for 15 minutes.

4. Meanwhile, cook the spaghetti according to the instructions on the package.

5. Serve topped with plenty of freshly grated Parmesan cheese and garnished with some flat-leaf parsley if desired.

Lang's Fried Asparagus in a Honey and Walnut Sauce

Featuring Lang Pinot Gris

Lang winemaker Bernhard Schirrmeister has shared this wonderful, flavourful recipe for asparagus, which uses the delightful Lang Pinot Gris. Asparagus is notoriously hard to pair wines with so by including the wine in the cooking process, a match is almost guaranteed. With asparagus growing wild throughout the Okanagan, you may even be able to pick yourself a fresh bunch. This dish also makes a great appetizer, and for non-vegetarians you could add a little prosciutto.

Serves 6-8 as a side

INGREDIENTS

½ cup olive oil
¾ cup chopped walnuts
¼ cup honey
3 tbsp Dijon mustard
2 tbsp white wine vinegar

1 tsp fresh chopped rosemary
salt and freshly ground black pepper
2 lb asparagus, woody ends removed
¼ cup white wine

1. Drizzle 1 tbsp of oil over the walnuts on a baking tray and place them under the broiler for about 2-3 minutes, flipping once and watching carefully to ensure that they do not burn. Remove from the oven and set aside. In a small bowl, combine the honey, mustard, vinegar, rosemary and salt and pepper to taste, stirring into a paste. Stir in the walnuts and set aside.

2. Heat the remaining oil in a large pan with a lid over medium-high heat. Fry the asparagus for 2 minutes, season with salt and pepper, then add the wine.

3. Reduce the heat to medium and cook for 4-5 minutes, stirring occasionally, before covering the pan with the lid for 2 minutes. Remove the lid, add the walnut mix and simmer for 2 minutes.

4. Serve immediately, accompanied by your favourite main dish and a glass of Lang Pinot Gris.

Pan-Fried Sweet Corn with Red Onion and Tomatoes

This simple combination of vegetables works beautifully with the wine and vinegar. As the Mayan and Aztec peoples have known for centuries, corn, onion and tomatoes taste great together. This side dish makes a great addition to any meal; we love it with roast chicken on wine-country picnics.

Serves 4-6 as a side

INGREDIENTS

3 ears fresh corn
2½ tbsp butter
1 small red onion, chopped
½ cup white wine

1 tbsp white wine vinegar
4 medium tomatoes, diced
salt and freshly ground black pepper

1. Peel the corn and remove all of the kernels from the cob with a sharp knife. Discard the cobs and set the kernels aside.

2. Melt the butter in a large pan over medium-high heat. Add the corn and onion and sauté for 4 minutes. Add the wine and vinegar and cook for an additional 6 minutes, until the liquid is almost completely evaporated.

3. Remove from the heat and set aside to cool. When the mixture has cooled, add the chopped tomatoes and stir well. Season to taste with salt and pepper and serve at room temperature.

Wine-Glazed Carrots

In this dish, the wine and vegetable stock provide depth of flavour while the butter and sugar give us a lovely, light caramelized glazing that makes this side dish absolutely irresistible.

Serves 4-6 as a side

INGREDIENTS

8 medium carrots, peeled and sliced
   into coins
¼ cup white wine
¼ cup vegetable stock

3 tbsp sugar
1 tbsp butter
salt and freshly ground black pepper

1. In a covered saucepan over medium-high heat, bring the carrots, wine, stock and 1½ tbsp of sugar to a boil. Reduce the heat to medium and simmer covered for about 5 minutes, stirring occasionally, until the carrots just begin to soften.

2. Remove the lid and turn the temperature up to high. Allow the liquid to reduce for about 2 minutes, until there are only a couple tbsp of liquid left.

3. Add the butter and remaining 1½ tbsp of sugar. Stir until the carrots are tender and ready for serving, about 2 minutes. Season with salt and black pepper to taste.

Perfect Greek-Style Oven-Roasted Potatoes

All over the world the Greeks are known for their delicious lemony potatoes. Now you can recreate this Mediterranean dish in the comfort of your own home. For an extra tasty treat, you could crumble some feta cheese over top before serving.

Serves 8 as a side

INGREDIENTS

8-10 medium potatoes, peeled and cut into 6 wedges

5 garlic cloves, crushed

¾ cup white wine

¾ cup water

juice from 1 large lemon

1 tbsp dried oregano

⅓ cup olive oil

salt and freshly ground black pepper

1. Preheat the oven to 450°F. Add the potatoes, garlic, wine, water, lemon juice and oregano to a large greased baking pan. Drizzle the olive oil over top and stir well to coat the spuds. Season with salt and pepper before placing the pan in the oven.

2. Bake for 45 minutes, then flip the potatoes. If the liquid dries up, then add a bit more water. Bake for another 40 minutes, or until the potatoes are golden and crispy. Serve as a side with your favourite Greek dish.

Golden Baked Onion Gratin

This is a side dish that you don't often see these days and we cannot figure out why. It is very rich, but it is well worth taking in a few additional calories to enjoy this fabulous treat.

Serves 6 as a side

INGREDIENTS

2 tbsp butter

6 medium onions, sliced

1 cup red wine

½ tsp nutmeg

¼ cup whipping cream

salt and freshly ground black pepper

1½ cups grated Swiss cheese

¼ cup grated Parmesan cheese

1. Preheat the oven to 375°F. Melt the butter in a large frying pan over medium-high heat and sauté the onions until softened, about 8 minutes. You may need to do this in batches.

2. Remove the onions from the pan and add the wine. Allow the liquid to reduce by about half.

3. Transfer the onions and the reduced wine to a baking dish and stir through the nutmeg and cream. Add salt and pepper to taste before topping with the cheese. Bake for 15-20 minutes until the cheese is golden brown.

Vegetarian & Side Dishes

Sauces & Marinades

I feel sorry for people who don't drink. When they wake up in the morning
that's as good as they are going to feel all day.

Frank Sinatra 1915-1998

Blue Mountain's Morel and Miso Sauce

Featuring Blue Mountain Pinot Gris

This wonderful recipe was conceived by Chef Geoffrey Couper, also known as the "Corked Cook". A few straightforward ingredients and a long simmer make a simple yet spectacular sauce for pasta or proteins. The deep earthy flavours of the miso stock echo the terroir of the Pinot Gris and the wild mushrooms. If you can't get fresh morels, try the farmers market, or you can substitute for any of the abundant tasty mushrooms we are blessed to have in BC, including chanterelles, boletus or puffballs. Miso paste is commonly available in the refrigerated section of the supermarket.

Yields 2-3 cups

INGREDIENTS

2 tbsp butter
3 large shallots, finely chopped
2 garlic cloves, finely chopped
2 big handfuls fresh morels, quartered
1 cup Pinot Gris
5 tbsp miso paste

2 cups warm water
1 tbsp soy sauce
2 cups whipping cream
white pepper
few drops lemon juice
¼ bunch fresh chives, finely sliced

1. Heat the butter in a medium-sized, heavy-bottomed pot over medium heat. Sauté the shallots and garlic stirring frequently until soft and translucent, but not browned, about 2 minutes. Add the mushrooms and continue to sauté for 3-4 minutes, until tender.

2. Add the Pinot Gris and simmer until reduced by half, about 5 minutes. While the wine reduces, whisk together the miso paste and warm water to make a simple miso stock. Add the miso stock and soy sauce to the mushroom mix and cook over medium heat to reduce the volume by half, about 25 minutes.

3. Add the whipping cream and cook the whole sauce down until it reaches a desirable, sauce-like consistency, about 25 minutes.

4. Season to taste with white pepper. Finish the sauce with a few drops of lemon juice and fresh chives, then serve over your favourite protein or pasta with a glass of Blue Mountain Pinot Gris.

Ruby Tuesday's Shiraz Sauce

Featuring Ruby Tuesday Shiraz

This tasty sauce from Ruby Tuesday makes a wonderful accompaniment to any red meat, although it was created especially with lamb in mind. Shiraz is the perfect flavour base, as the pepper and dark berry fruit characteristics of the wine blend with the beef stock to make a rich, smooth sauce that brings out the best in any red meat.

Serves 4-6 with lamb

INGREDIENTS

3 tbsp cold unsalted butter, cut into pieces
¼ cup finely chopped shallots
⅓ cup Shiraz
1 cup beef stock

3 sprigs fresh rosemary
3 sprigs fresh thyme
2 tbsp tomato paste
½ tsp sugar
salt and freshly ground black pepper

1. Melt 1 tbsp of the butter in a sauté pan over medium heat, add the shallots and sauté until they are translucent, about 3 minutes.

2. Turn up the heat to medium-high and add the Shiraz. Bring to a boil, then reduce the wine until there are only 2-3 tbsp left. Add the beef stock, fresh herbs, tomato paste and sugar, then bring to a boil and reduce until the sauce is thick enough to coat the back of a wooden spoon.

3. Remove from the heat, then whisk in the remaining 2 tbsp of butter, until it has melted and the sauce has thickened. Season to taste with salt and pepper. Spoon the sauce over cooked lamb and serve with boiled baby potatoes, steamed vegetables and a glass of Ruby Tuesday Shiraz.

D'Angelo's Setta Coppa Pasta Sauce

Featuring D'Angelo Estate Winery Setta Coppa

Winemaker Sal D'Angelo has created this divine pasta sauce, made in the tradition of Abruzzi, Italy, using his Bordeaux-style Setta Coppa wine. Sal was inspired to cook by his mother, Rosalina, who had 4 boys and no girls to teach her cooking secrets to. Many people worry about using anchovies in cooking because they do not like the taste of them on their own, but in this dish the taste is not too fishy and the anchovies give the sauce a simple richness.

Serves 4 with pasta

INGREDIENTS

4 tbsp olive oil

1 sweet white onion, finely chopped

2 garlic cloves, finely chopped

1 can chopped plum tomatoes (19 oz)

1 tsp tomato paste

1 can anchovies

1 cup red wine

1 tsp dried basil (or 3 fresh leaves)

1. Add 3 tbsp of olive oil and onions to a large pan over medium heat. Cook, stirring occasionally, until just before the onion turns golden brown. Add the garlic and stir for 45 seconds.

2. Add the tomatoes and tomato paste, bring to a boil, then reduce the heat and simmer for 20 minutes.

3. In a small pan over medium heat, combine the anchovies with 1 tbsp of olive oil. Stir gently until the anchovies dissolve.

4. Add the anchovy oil to the simmering sauce. Add the wine and the basil and simmer until the sauce has thickened, about 20 minutes.

5. Serve over al dente pasta and enjoy with a glass of D'Angelo Setta Coppa.

Raspberry and Blue Cheese Dipping Sauce

Raspberries are a home-grown fruit that we get plenty of in BC. This simple dip uses the sweet, tart flavour of the fruit complemented by the wine and contrasts it with the saltiness of the blue cheese to create a mouth-watering dip that is bursting with flavour. You can substitute the raspberry jam for other jams with similar results. We've used peach, strawberry and even fig jams to make this masterpiece.

Serves 4-6 with bread

INGREDIENTS

¼ cup balsamic vinegar

¼ cup raspberry jam

2 tbsp red wine or port-style wine

¼ cup crumbled blue cheese

1 garlic clove, crushed

salt and freshly ground black pepper

½ cup olive oil

1. Mix all of the ingredients except the olive oil together in a bowl and stir well.

2. Slowly whisk in the olive oil until it is thoroughly combined. Cover and refrigerate for at least 2-3 hours before serving.

3. Remove from the refrigerator and give it a quick mix before serving in a bowl placed on a tray, surrounded by slices of baguette or focaccia.

Pineapple, Mango and Kiwi Salsa

This taste of the tropics makes a wonderful addition to all sorts of grilled dishes including fish, prawns, pork or chicken. It's easy to make and the only part that is time consuming is the chopping. It's perfect to bring to a summer BBQ. You can adjust the amount of jalapeño pepper to taste.

Serves 4-6 as a side

INGREDIENTS

2 cups chopped fresh pineapple
1 mango, chopped
2 kiwis, peeled and chopped
¼ cup chopped fresh cilantro

1 tbsp grated ginger
2 tbsp off-dry Gewürztraminer (or Riesling)
1 tbsp chopped jalapeño pepper

1. Mix all of the ingredients together in a bowl and allow to sit for at least 1 hour covered in the fridge before serving.

Homemade Cranberry Sauce

This sauce makes a great accompaniment to your holiday turkey or chicken dinner and it works equally well on turkey burgers. It is easy to make and much tastier than canned varieties.

Yields 1½ cups

INGREDIENTS

½ cup red wine
½ cup orange juice
1 tsp grated ginger

1 cup sugar
3 cups cranberries (fresh or frozen)

1. Place the wine, orange juice, ginger and sugar in a medium-sized pan over medium-high heat. Stir until the sugar dissolves and bring to a rapid boil.

2. Add the cranberries and cook until they pop, about 5 minutes. Reduce the heat to a gentle simmer and keep cooking, stirring occasionally, until the sauce has thickened, about 20-25 minutes. Let the sauce cool completely in the refrigerator before serving.

Classic Chardonnay Sauce

This classic Chardonnay sauce can be served over chicken, fish, potatoes, rice, or pretty much anything that needs a rich flavour boost. It was adapted from a recipe by Executive Chef Jason Parsons from Peller Estates who used the Peller Private Reserve Chardonnay to create this classic.

Yields ¾ cup

INGREDIENTS

½ tbsp butter
1 tbsp finely sliced shallots
1 garlic clove, crushed
½ cup Chardonnay

¼ cup chicken stock
¼ bunch fresh thyme, chopped
2 cups whipping cream
salt and freshly ground black pepper

1. Melt the butter in a saucepan over medium heat. Sweat the shallots and garlic for about 1-2 minutes, being careful not to brown. Add the wine and allow to reduce by half. Add the chicken stock and allow the liquid to reduce by half again.

2. Add the thyme and the cream and reduce the mixture by about ⅔. Strain then season with salt and pepper and serve over your meal.

Japanese Steak Sauce

This Japanese-style steak sauce is also fantastic served on its own over plain white rice. The black sesame seeds are the key ingredient and they can usually be found in the Asian section of the supermarket.

Yields 2½-3 cups

INGREDIENTS

¾ cup black sesame seeds
1⅓ cups olive oil
½ cup soy sauce

½ cup red wine
½ cup chopped white onion
1 tbsp Dijon mustard

1. Combine all of the ingredients in a blender or food processor and blend until smooth and creamy. Serve at room temperature or slightly heated over steak or plain rice.

Basic Red Wine BBQ Marinade

This recipe is very simple, but it works incredibly well for all types of red meat. You can adjust it to suit your own tastes by using different herbs; rosemary, tarragon and oregano make excellent additions. If you are cooking prime cuts of meats, then substitute the soy sauce for some Worcestershire sauce for a more subtle flavour.

Yields 1¼ cups

INGREDIENTS

1 cup red wine

4 garlic cloves, chopped

¼ cup soy sauce

¼ cup chopped fresh thyme

1. Combine all of the ingredients in a resealable plastic bag or a covered non-reactive dish.

2. Add the red meat of your choice, cover and refrigerate for at least 4 hours, but preferably overnight.

White Wine Marinade for Fish and Seafood

This is another basic recipe, but the results are delicious. The lime juice provides a zesty finish to the delicate wine flavours. The marinade does not have too many strong flavours so it will not overwhelm the fish or seafood. If you do feel like spicing it up a little, add some Tabasco or a chopped jalapeño to the marinade before adding the fish.

Yields ¾ cup

INGREDIENTS

½ cup dry white wine

¼ cup olive oil

2 tbsp lime juice

1 green onion, chopped

1 garlic clove, crushed

1 tsp salt

½ tsp ground black pepper

1. Combine all of the ingredients in a resealable plastic bag or a covered non-reactive dish.

2. Add the fish or seafood and ensure that it is completely covered in the marinade. Refrigerate for about 30 minutes, but definitely no more than 2 hours, or the citrus will start cooking the fish. You can baste the seafood with excess marinade while cooking, but be sure to stop basting during the last 5 minutes of cooking. This will ensure that any raw fish juices in the marinade are thoroughly cooked.

Marinade for Eastern-Style Kebabs

This marinade is awesome for beef or lamb kebabs. As usual, the trick is to ensure you leave enough marinating time for the flavours to work their way into the meat. Just before cooking, thread the meat onto skewers and grill on a hot BBQ. Try serving with pita, sliced tomatoes and tzatziki.

Yields 1¼ cups

INGREDIENTS

2 tbsp olive oil

1 tbsp balsamic vinegar

1 cup red wine

4 garlic cloves, crushed

¾ tsp ground cumin

¾ tsp ground coriander

½ tsp cayenne

¼ tsp salt

1. Combine all of the ingredients in a resealable plastic bag or a covered non-reactive dish. Add about 1½ lb of lamb or beef chopped into 1½-inch pieces and mix thoroughly.

2. Allow the marinade to work its magic for at least 12 hours in the refrigerator, turning every few hours.

Garlic and Thyme Marinade for Chicken

Although this was created as a marinade for chicken, it works equally well with other poultry dishes.

Yeilds 1 cup

INGREDIENTS

5 large garlic cloves, crushed

¼ cup dry white wine

¼ cup lemon juice

2 tbsp chopped fresh thyme

1 tsp paprika

½ tsp cayenne pepper

1 tsp salt

1 tsp freshly ground black pepper

½ cup olive oil

1. Combine all of the ingredients in a resealable plastic bag or a covered non-reactive dish.

2. Add the poultry, making sure that it is well coated in the marinade, then refrigerate for up to 6 hours. You can use the excess marinade to baste the chicken while cooking, but be sure to stop basting at least 5 minutes prior to removing the chicken from the heat.

Desserts

Never spare the parson's wine nor the baker's pudding.
Benjamin Franklin 1706-1790

Inniskillin Summer Berries with Chilled Icewine Cream

Featuring Inniskillin Okanagan Riesling

This recipe was created by the late Executive Chef Izabela Kalabis-Sacco, who was resident chef at Inniskillin's Niagara location 1988-2006. The rich cream is a wonderful contrast to the vibrant acidity of the Riesling Icewine. This elegant yet simple recipe has all the elements of a classic and it will prove timeless. This recipe is perfect for finishing the last bit of Icewine in the bottle. For extra extravagance Chef Kalabis-Sacco suggested soaking the berries in a little additional Icewine.

Serves 4

INGREDIENTS

3 egg yolks
½ cup sugar
⅓ cup Icewine
½ cup whipping cream

3 cups mixed berries (strawberries, blueberries, raspberries, etc.)
fresh mint or lavender for garnish

1. In a small saucepan over low heat, whisk together the egg yolks, sugar and Icewine until thickened. Remove from the heat and continue to whisk until it starts to cool. Chill the mixture in the refrigerator for 1 hour.

2. In a separate bowl, whip the cream until soft peaks form. Fold the cream into the Icewine mixture and chill for at least 30 minutes.

3. Place the berries into individual bowls or large wine glasses. Top each with a large spoonful of Icewine cream and garnish with fresh mint or lavender.

Isabella's Vanilla Cheesecake with a Fruit Wine Reduction

Featuring Isabella Winery Raspberry Wine

This fabulous, rich vanilla cheesecake recipe from Isabella Winery is topped with a delightful fruit wine reduction. Although raspberry wine was the first choice for this recipe, you can also use other sweet fruit wines such as blueberry or cherry to achieve equally pleasing results. The cheesecake can be prepared up to two days in advance.

Serves 6-8

INGREDIENTS

1½ cups graham cracker crumbs

1½ cups + 2 tbsp sugar

½ tsp ground cinnamon

¼ cup melted butter, cooled

2 lb cream cheese, at room temperature

2 tbsp all-purpose flour

¼ tsp salt

½ cup sour cream

1 tsp vanilla extract

3 large eggs, at room temperature

1½ cups sweet fruit wine

½ cinnamon stick

zest from ¼ orange

1. Preheat the oven to 400°F and lightly butter a 9-inch springform pan.
In a bowl, stir together the crumbs, 2 tbsp of sugar, ground cinnamon and butter until well blended. Cover your hand with plastic wrap to form a glove, and evenly and firmly press the crumbs over the bottom of the pan. Bake the crust for 10 minutes or until it is golden brown. Remove it from the oven and allow it to cool. Reduce the oven temperature to 300°F.

2. While the crust is baking, start preparing the filling. In a large bowl, combine the cream cheese, flour and salt, using an electric mixer on medium-high speed for 4 minutes, until smooth and creamy. Add 1¼ cups of sugar, sour cream and vanilla and continue beating until smooth, about 3 minutes. Add the eggs one at a time, beating well after each addition and occasionally scraping down the sides of the bowl, until the mixture is smooth and creamy.

3. Pour the filling into the prepared pan, spreading the mixture evenly. Bake for about 70 minutes, until the filling is just set (it will still be a little loose in the center). Transfer the pan to a wire rack and let the cheesecake cool to room temperature, at least 1 hour, then refrigerate until well chilled, at least 4 hours.

4. To make the sauce, combine the wine and remaining ¼ cup of sugar, cinnamon stick and zest in a medium-sized saucepan over medium heat. Bring to a simmer, stirring to dissolve the sugar, then increase the heat to high and reduce to ¾ cup. Taste and add more sugar if desired. Remove the zest and cinnamon stick and discard. Allow the sauce to cool.

5. To serve, run a knife around the pan sides to loosen the cake. Release the pan sides, then cut the cake into slices and spoon the fruit wine reduction sauce over each slice. You may also like to top the cake with some fresh fruit.

Seven Stones' Pear Custard Flan with Rosé Sauce

Featuring Seven Stones Pinot Rosé

The team at Seven Stones have provided the keys to this easy-to-make, scrumptious fruit dessert. The pears are lightly caramelized in a pan with butter and sugar before being incorporated into a delicious custard-based flan and topped with a Rosé wine sauce. If you do not have fresh pears you can also use canned pears for this wonderful dessert.

Serves 6

INGREDIENTS

2 tbsp butter

5 pears, peeled, cored and cut into 6 wedges

6 tbsp sugar

1 tbsp all-purpose flour

1 pinch ground nutmeg

4 large eggs

1½ cups half-and-half cream

1 tsp vanilla

1 cup + 3 tbsp Rosé

¼ tsp lemon rind (optional)

pinch ground cinnamon

1½ tsp cornstarch

⅓ cup fruit jelly

1. Preheat the oven to 350°F. Melt the butter in frying pan over medium heat and add the pears and 2 tbsp of sugar. Sauté until the pears begin to turn a light gold colour, about 10 minutes. Transfer the pears to a 9-inch round baking dish.

2. In a bowl, combine 2 tbsp of sugar, flour, nutmeg, eggs, cream and vanilla. Mix until well blended, then pour the mixture over top of the pears. Bake for 40 minutes or until a knife inserted in the centre comes out clean. Allow to cool at room temperature.

3. While the mixture is baking, make the sauce by combining 1 cup of Rosé, 2 tbsp of sugar, lemon rind and cinnamon in a small saucepan over medium-high heat. Bring to a boil, then reduce the heat to a simmer. In a cup, combine the cornstarch and 3 tbsp of wine and mix until smooth. Add the cornstarch mixture and the jelly into the saucepan and stir to combine. Allow the mixture to simmer until the sauce thickens, about 10 minutes. Set aside to cool.

4. To serve, cut the pear flan into wedges and serve topped with the cooled sauce. This dish is divine with vanilla ice cream.

Paradise on Ice

Featuring Paradise Ranch Riesling Icewine

This delectable dessert is very quick to prepare. The recipe was created by Allison Boulton, Paradise Ranch Director of Operations. She was inspired while serving Riesling Icewine to her family and by combining ice cream, warm roasted almonds and chocolate shavings, she created this true taste of paradise. You could also use a sweet late-harvest wine to recreate this dish.

Serves 4

INGREDIENTS

½ cup sliced almonds
8 scoops vanilla ice cream
¼-½ cup Icewine

⅓ cup dark chocolate shavings (or
   your favourite chocolate)

1. Preheat the oven to 350°F. Spread the almonds on a baking sheet and toast until lightly browned, stirring once, about 10 minutes. Watch them very carefully to ensure that they do not burn.

2. Place 2 scoops of ice cream into each serving bowl, then pour the Icewine over top. The amount used depends on your sweet tooth. Top with toasted almonds and chocolate shavings and serve immediately while the almonds are still warm.

Raven Ridge Butterscotch Apple Crepes

Featuring Raven Ridge Iced Gala Apple Cider

Award-winning Chef Travis Hackl from the Ridge Restaurant created this masterpiece that provides a wonderful finish to any meal. To save some time, you can prepare the luscious pastry cream in advance. This recipe is heavenly when served with vanilla ice cream and fresh mint.

Serves 4

INGREDIENTS

3 egg yolks	2 tbsp butter + 1 tsp melted butter
⅓ cup + 1 tbsp sugar	1 tsp oil
⅔ cup + 1 tbsp all-purpose flour, sifted	1 cup brown sugar, packed
½ tbsp cornstarch	2 oz sweet apple cider
1 cup milk	2 apples, peeled, cored and diced
1 tsp vanilla	¼ tsp ground cinnamon
1 egg, beaten	½ cup whipping cream
3 tbsp water	fresh mint leaves for garnish

1. To make the pastry cream, beat the egg yolks, ⅓ cup of granulated sugar, 1 tbsp of flour and cornstarch until the mixture is well combined and pale yellow. In a saucepan over medium heat, scald ½ cup of milk and vanilla, stirring frequently, until it begins to steam and small bubbles appear around the edge of the saucepan. Do not boil. Slowly stir through the egg yolk mixture and remove from the heat. Strain the mixture into a into a small saucepan over medium heat. Stir constantly until the mixture boils and thickens. Transfer to a bowl, cover and cool.

2. To make the crepe batter, mix together the remaining ⅔ cup of sifted flour with the beaten egg, ½ cup of milk, water, 1 tsp of melted butter, oil and remaining 1 tbsp of granulated sugar until they form a smooth batter.

3. To make the crepes, heat a non-stick pan over medium heat and add enough batter to make a thin 5-inch circle. Flip after the batter firms up and cook for 1 minute. Repeat the process, making 16 crepes.

4. To make the butterscotch apples, combine the brown sugar, cider, 2 tbsp of butter, apples and cinnamon in a small saucepan over medium heat. Bring to a boil and simmer for 1 minute, then add the cream, set aside and keep warm.

5. To assemble, fold each crepe in half twice, creating a cone-shaped pocket. Fill the crepe pockets with pastry cream and place 4 crepes on each plate. Top with the butterscotch apples and serve with a scoop of vanilla ice cream. This dish looks great garnished with fresh mint leaves.

Cabernet Chocolate Cupcakes

Wine and chocolate are both lavish treats that are rarely savoured together. Here we not only include a dense Cabernet Sauvignon in the rich batter of the cupcake, but also in the luscious chocolaty-maple icing that tops these decadent delights. The trick is to use good quality chocolate.

Makes about 24 cupcakes

INGREDIENTS

3 cups all-purpose flour
1 tbsp baking powder
2 cups sugar
½ tsp salt
½ cup cocoa powder
6 eggs
1¾ cups Cabernet Sauvignon

1 tsp vanilla extract
½ cup vegetable oil
2 cups dark chocolate chips
7 oz sweetened condensed milk
¼ cup maple syrup
2 tsp balsamic vinegar

1. Preheat the oven to 350°F. Line 2 cupcake pans with paper cupcake holders.

2. In a large mixing bowl, sift together the flour, baking powder, sugar, salt and cocoa. Make a well in the middle of the dry ingredients and add the eggs, 1½ cups of wine, vanilla and oil. With an electric mixer on a low speed, mix into a lump-free batter.

3. In a double boiler (or you can improvise with a heat-safe bowl over a pan of boiling water), melt 1 cup of chocolate chips, stirring constantly. Pour the melted chocolate into the batter and stir through. Fill each paper cupcake holder just below the top.

4. Bake for about 25 minutes, until the cupcakes are firm to touch. They should have risen over the top. Remove from the oven to cool.

5. Combine the remaining cup of chocolate chips, condensed milk, remaining ¼ cup of wine, maple syrup and vinegar in a microwavable bowl and microwave on high for two minutes. Stir well so that you have a fairly runny mixture. Alternatively, if you don't have a microwave, combine the ingredients in a saucepan over medium-low heat, stirring constantly until the ingredients are well combined.

6. Allow the mixture to cool slightly and thicken and then dip the tops of each cupcake into the mixture. Allow the topping to harden slightly on the cupcakes and then dip them a second time to create a thicker topping. Enjoy with a glass of Cabernet Sauvignon.

Okanagan Peach Cobbler

Fresh Okanagan peaches are a highlight of any BC summer. Although many of the Okanagan orchards have been converted to vineyards, there is still an abundance of fresh orchard fruit grown throughout the Okanagan. Make sure you stop in at one of the many roadside fruit stands if you are driving through during the summer months, as the incredible selection of locally grown produce is often cheaper and far fresher than you could find in a supermarket.

Serves 6

INGREDIENTS

3-4 large peaches, sliced
1½ cups sugar
⅓ cup late harvest wine
1 cup all-purpose flour
2 tsp baking powder

¼ tsp salt
⅔ cup milk
1 egg
⅓ cup melted butter
1 tsp ground cinnamon

1. Preheat the oven to 350°F. In a large bowl, soak the sliced peaches in ½ cup of sugar and the late harvest wine.

2. In a separate bowl, mix together the flour, remaining 1 cup of sugar, baking powder and salt. Stir in the milk and egg and mix well.

3. Pour the melted butter into the bottom of a 9x13-inch baking pan. Pour the batter on top of the melted butter.

4. Layer the peaches on top of the batter so that the top is covered in fruit. Pour any remaining wine from the bowl over top and sprinkle with the cinnamon.

5. Bake for about 45 minutes until the batter is a lovely golden brown colour. Serve hot with a scoop of vanilla ice cream.

Marichel's Syrah Ganache Brownies

Featuring Marichel Vineyard Syrah

This decadent version of a much loved classic was created by Marichel winemaker Richard Roskell. You have never tasted brownies like this! The Syrah also makes a wonderful accompaniment to the chocolate and cherries so feel free to indulge in a glass as you devour these delicious treats. These brownies are also great for freezing.

Serves 12

INGREDIENTS

½ cup chopped dried cherries

⅓ + ½ cup syrah

1 cup butter

2 cups sugar

4 large eggs

½ tsp vanilla extract

⅔ cup all-purpose flour

¾ cup unsweetened cocoa powder

½ tsp baking powder

½ tsp salt

½ cup whipping cream

6 oz semisweet chocolate, finely chopped

1. In a small saucepan, bring the cherries and ⅓ cup of wine to a boil over medium heat. Reduce the heat to low and simmer for 2 minutes. Remove the pan from the heat and let the cherries cool to room temperature. Position a rack in the center of the oven and preheat to 350°F. Lightly butter and flour a 9x13-inch metal baking pan, tapping out the excess flour.

2. Melt the butter in a medium-sized saucepan over medium heat. Remove from the heat and stir in the sugar, followed by the eggs and vanilla. Add the flour, cocoa, baking powder and salt, stirring until the batter is smooth. Stir in the wine-soaked cherries, along with any remaining wine. Spread the batter evenly in the prepared baking pan. Bake for about 40 minutes, or until an inserted tester comes out clean. Cool the brownies on a rack.

3. To make the ganache topping, bring the remaining ½ cup of wine to a boil in a small saucepan over medium heat. Reduce to 2 tbsp, then pour it into a cup and reserve. Thoroughly rinse the pan. Bring the whipping cream to a boil in the saucepan over medium-high heat, stirring occasionally. Remove from the heat as soon as it boils, stir in the chopped chocolate and reduced wine and mix until the mixture is smooth and the chocolate has melted.

4. Pour the ganache into a bowl and cover to prevent a skin from forming. Cool to room temperature, stirring occasionally, then spread evenly over the cooled brownies and allow to set for 1 hour. Cut into 12 squares and serve.

Sea Cider Rumrunner Bread Pudding

Featuring Sea Cider Rumrunner Cider

This incredible bread pudding recipe was the winner of Sea Cider's First Annual Cider Cook-Off. Infused with Rumrunner, a cider aged in old rum barrels, this bread pudding makes a delightful dessert out of stale bread. The use of eggnog and cinnamon make this a perfect Christmas treat. For the best results, this recipe should be prepared a day in advance to give the flavours plenty of time to infuse into the bread.

Serves 6

INGREDIENTS

4 cups day-old croissants or brioche
   bread, broken into 2-inch pieces
3 large eggs + 5 large egg yolks
2 cups eggnog
1½ cups sparkling cider
1 cup whipping cream
¼ cup butter + 1 tbsp melted butter

½ cup packed dark brown sugar
½ tsp ground cinnamon
½ tsp nutmeg
1 tart apple (eg. Granny Smith)
   peeled, cored and chopped
½ cup chopped dried apples
½ cup sugar

1. Grease 2 loaf pans with butter and fill with the croissant pieces. In a mixing bowl, beat together 3 large eggs, eggnog, 1 cup of sparkling cider, whipping cream, 1 tbsp of melted butter, brown sugar, cinnamon and nutmeg. Pour the mixture over the croissants. Mix in the fresh and dried apples and stir so the liquid is absorbed. Cover and refrigerate overnight.

2. Remove from the fridge prior to baking and let it sit to bring to room temperature. Preheat the oven to 350°F and bake for 1 hour.

3. While the pudding is baking make the sauce. Melt ¼ cup of butter in a double boiler (or improvise with a heat-safe bowl over a saucepan of boiling water). Whisk in the sugar until it is combined, then add ½ cup of cider and whisk for another 2 minutes. Remove from the simmering water entirely and add the 5 egg yolks, one at a time, until well mixed. Return to the top of the simmering water. Continue whisking until the mixture pales and thickens, about 5-7 minutes. Keep the sauce warm over the hot water, but off the element, until the pudding is ready. As the sauce cools it will thicken more.

4. As soon as the pudding is ready, top with the sauce and serve immediately.

Gewürztraminer Summer Fruit Salad

Sometimes there is nothing better for dessert than a fruit salad. This recipe uses Gewürztraminer to spice it up and give it an extra dimension, but you could also use a Riesling. You can adapt this salad with your favourite fruits or whatever is in season. It's best made ahead of time as it takes a while to cool the sauce and the longer the fruit soaks up the wine sauce, the more delicious it becomes.

Serves 8

INGREDIENTS

½ cup Gewürztraminer
½ cup orange juice
¼ cup brown sugar
1 cinnamon stick
1 bunch grapes

2 oranges, peeled and sectioned
3 kiwis, peeled and sliced
2 bananas sliced
2 mangos, peeled and cut into pieces
1 punnet strawberries, halved

1. In a saucepan over medium-high heat, combine the wine, orange juice, sugar and cinnamon stick. Bring to a boil, then allow to simmer for 5-6 minutes. Remove from the heat and transfer the mixture to the fridge to cool.

2. Meanwhile, mix together the fruit in a large glass bowl. When the wine mixture has cooled, remove the cinnamon stick, pour the mixture over top of the fruit and toss. Return the fruit salad to the fridge to chill until you are ready to serve. Toss before serving on its own or with whipped cream, yogurt or ice cream.

Blueberry Cinnamon Cake in Minutes

This is the perfect cake to prepare if you are short on time. It is very simple to make; it can literally be thrown together in just minutes. The fresh blueberries give it a burst of wonderful goodness. British Columbia is one of the highest producers of blueberries in the world and there are more than 650 commercial growers with over 17,000 acres planted. Every year, more than 80 million pounds of blueberries are farmed in this province alone! The blueberry wine can be substituted for any dessert-style fruit wine or grape wine.

Serves 8

INGREDIENTS

2 cups all-purpose flour	1 tsp vanilla extract
1¼ cups sugar	¼ cup blueberry wine
2½ tsp baking powder	2 cups blueberries
¼ tsp salt	½ cup brown sugar
1 egg	2 tsp ground cinnamon
1 cup milk	¼ cup melted butter

1. Preheat the oven to 350°F. In a large mixing bowl, mix the flour, granulated sugar, baking powder and salt. When the mixture is well combined, add the egg, milk vanilla and blueberry wine and stir until just combined. Add the blueberries, gently folding them into the mixture.

2. Pour the batter into a greased 9x13-inch baking pan, then sprinkle the brown sugar and cinnamon over top. Pour the melted butter over top and bake for 30 minutes. Remove from the oven and allow to cool slightly before serving warm with vanilla ice cream.

Tugwell Creek Farm's Lavender Honey Cheesecake

Featuring Tugwell Creek Farm's Sack Mead-Wassail Gold

Cooking with lavender is really catching on and through this delicious, light cheesecake created by Tugwell Creek Farm you can experience the pleasure for yourself. Do not use lavender that comes directly from florists or garden stores, as they may have been sprayed with pesticides. The lovely sweet sack mead is a wonderful addition to this delightful dish, but you can also use honey if you can't find the mead.

Serves 6-8

INGREDIENTS

½ lb shortbread cookies (or graham crackers), crushed into crumbs

5 tbsp melted butter

2 tbsp boiling water

2 tbsp sweet mead (or 2 tsp honey)

3 tbsp lavender petals, tied in cheesecloth

8 oz light cream cheese

½ cup wildflower honey

1½ cups whipping cream

lavender flowers for garnish

1. Place the cookie crumbs in a bowl and mix with the melted butter. Press this mixture into the bottom of a 9-inch springform pan and place it in the refrigerator for 1 hour.

2. To make the lavender infusion pour the boiling water and the mead into a small bowl and add the lavender satchel, soaking it for 15 minutes. Remove the lavender satchel after squeezing it gently to extract any liquid, then let the mixture cool.

3. In a large bowl, beat together the cream cheese and honey until smooth. Gradually add the lavender infused liquid and keep beating until it is well combined and smooth.

4. In a small bowl, whip the cream until it forms soft peaks and then fold it into the cream cheese mixture. Pour the filling over the crumb base and place in the refrigerator for 3–4 hours to set.

5. Sprinkle the top with lavender flowers to garnish before serving. Run a warm knife around the inside edge of the springform pan. Release the pan sides, then slice and serve.

Chocolate Pudding Cakes with a Strawberry Riesling Coulis

These wonderful chocolate pudding cakes are served with a strawberry Riesling coulis that completes them perfectly. The Riesling provides complexity to the strawberry coulis and it works equally well with a dry or off-dry wine. It is advantageous to make the coulis an hour or so in advance so that it gets plenty of time to chill in the fridge.

Serves 8

INGREDIENTS

2 cups quartered strawberries

¼ cup Riesling

2 tbsp + 1 cup sugar

1 tsp fresh lemon juice

1 cup all-purpose flour

⅔ cup unsweetened cocoa powder

½ tsp baking powder

¾ tsp salt

2 large eggs

¾ cup whole milk

¼ cup melted butter, cooled

2 tsp vanilla extract

¾ cup firmly packed dark brown sugar

1½ cups boiling water

3 oz bittersweet chocolate, broken into small pieces

1. To make the coulis, combine the strawberries, wine, 2 tbsp of granulated sugar and the lemon juice in a blender or food processor and then blend until smooth. Cover and transfer to the fridge to chill.

2. Preheat the oven to 350°F. In a large bowl, sift together the flour, ⅓ cup of cocoa, baking powder and salt. Set aside.

3. Whisk together the eggs, 1 cup of granulated sugar, milk, melted butter and vanilla, then add this to the flour mixture. Stir until just combined and then pour the batter evenly among 8 individual-size ramekins.

4. In a medium-sized bowl, whisk together the remaining ⅓ cup of cocoa powder, brown sugar and boiling water. Pour the cocoa mixture evenly over top of the batter. Do not mix. Drop the chocolate pieces over top of the batter.

5. Bake for 25-30 minutes, or until an inserted tester comes out clean. Let the puddings cool for 10-15 minutes. Serve the puddings topped with the coulis and with whipped cream or ice cream on the side.

Sticky Date Pudding

This sticky date pudding just might be the greatest dessert of all time. It is loaded with delicious dates and topped with a warm butterscotch sauce that will melt your heart. This dish is already very popular in Australia and its only a matter of time before it makes its mark on menus across North America. The red wine gives the date pudding a wonderful depth and you could also use a port-styled wine for an even richer pudding.

Serves 6-8

INGREDIENTS

8 oz pitted dates	2 eggs
1½ cups red wine	1 cup all-purpose flour
1 tsp baking soda	1 tsp baking powder
1 cup butter	1 cup whipping cream
¾ cup sugar	1½ cups brown sugar

1. Preheat the oven to 350°F. In a saucepan over medium-high heat, bring the dates and wine to a boil. Stir in the baking soda and then remove from the heat. Allow the mixture to stand for about 10 minutes before transferring to a food processor. Blend and set aside.

2. Using an electric mixer on a slow speed, cream together ¼ cup of butter and the granulated sugar. Once the mixture is smooth, add the eggs, flour and baking powder and then fold in the date mixture until well combined. Transfer the batter to a greased 7-inch round cake pan and bake for about 55 minutes.

3. While the pudding is baking, combine the cream, brown sugar and remaining ¾ cup of butter in a saucepan over medium-high heat. Bring to a boil and then reduce the heat to a simmer, stirring frequently, for about 10 minutes.

4. When the pudding is done, remove it from the oven and let it rest for 5 minutes. Top with the butterscotch sauce then return it to the oven for another 5 minutes to allow the sauce to infuse into the pudding.

5. Serve with ice cream or whipped cream and be prepared to dish up seconds as one serving is rarely enough!

Vern Rose of House of Rose Vineyards during harvest.

House of Rose Winter Fruit Compote

Featuring House of Rose Chardonnay

Aura Rose at House of Rose Winery has come up with this fruity dessert that uses ingredients that are available in supermarkets year-round. The sweet flavours of the fruit make an excellent companion to the bright flavours displayed in the wine. You can always alter this recipe by adding different fresh fruits to the mix as they are in season.

Serves 6-8

INGREDIENTS

8 dried figs or dates
8 pitted prunes
8 dried apricots
½ cup seedless raisins
1 cup unsweetened apple juice
1 cup Chardonnay
1 cup water

¼ cup sugar
1 tsp grated lemon zest
2 tsp grated orange zest
2 apples, peeled, cored and cut into
  wedges
2 pears, peeled, cored and cut into
  wedges

1. Place the dried fruit in a small bowl and cover with apple juice. Allow the fruit to soak for 30-60 minutes.

2. In a medium-sized saucepan over high heat, combine the wine, water, sugar and zests. Stir well and bring to a boil. Add the presoaked fruit and reduce the heat to a simmer for 10 minutes, stirring occasionally.

3. Add the apples, cover and cook for 5 minutes. Add the pears, cover and cook for 5 minutes more. Remove from the heat, cover and for the best results allow to stand at room temperature for about 2 hours.

4. This dish can be served on its own, but it's also delicious with vanilla ice cream, gingerbread or lemon pound cake.

Starling Lane Blackberry Pepper Sorbet

Featuring Starling Lane Wild Blackberry Dessert Wine

This delightful sorbet was created by Sherry Mussio of Starling Lane Winery. Although the peppers make a delightful and tasty addition to the sorbet, it can also be made without them for those that don't like spice. The beauty of this dish is that you can easily make your own delicious sorbet without having to purchase an ice cream maker!

Serves 4

INGREDIENTS

¼ tsp dried red jalapeño peppers

1 cup blackberry dessert wine

2 cups frozen blackberries, defrosted

1 cup apple juice

1 cup berry sugar (ultra-fine sugar)

fresh mint leaves for garnish (optional)

1. Soak the jalapeño peppers in the dessert wine for an hour. In the meantime, purée the blackberries in a food processor and press through a fine sieve with a rubber spatula to remove the seeds. Discard the seeds.

2. Add the apple juice and sugar to the purée and stir until the sugar is completely dissolved. Add the wine and pepper mix and stir until it is well combined.

3. Pour the mixture into a shallow dish and freeze until firm. Remove from the freezer and purée in a food processor until smooth. Transfer to a container, cover with plastic wrap and freeze until it's set and ready to serve.

4. To serve, scoop the mixture into balls and place them in stemmed martini glasses that have been frosted in the freezer. For an elegant garnish top with a sprig of fresh mint.

Port-Infused Turtle Cubes

Every Christmas, turtle chocolates are a huge hit across North America. Now you can make your own version as squares, with a rich caramel toffee layer, a smooth chocolate topping and a base made with walnuts and a port-styled wine. You can also use port-styled fruit wine or red wine to make this tray of goodies. Just a warning, once you've made this recipe you'll be committed to a lifetime of baking these delicious turtle cubes.

Makes 24-30 squares

INGREDIENTS

1½ cups + 2 tbsp butter

1½ cups brown sugar

1¾ cups rolled oats

¾ cup all-purpose flour

¼ cup cocoa

½ cup port-styled wine

½ tsp baking soda

½ cup chopped walnuts

½ cup condensed milk

2 tbsp corn syrup

⅔ cup semisweet chocolate chips

1. Preheat the oven to 350°F. Melt 1 cup of butter in a medium-sized saucepan over medium heat. Add 1 cup of brown sugar, the rolled oats, flour, cocoa, wine, baking soda and walnuts. Stir together until well combined and the port is absorbed into the oats, about 3-4 minutes. Press the mixture into the bottom of a greased 9x13 inch pan. Bake uncovered for 15 minutes.

2. Meanwhile, combine the condensed milk, corn syrup, ½ cup of butter and the remaining ½ cup of brown sugar in a saucepan over medium heat. Allow the mixture to boil gently for 5 minutes, stirring continuously to avoid burning. Remove from the heat and whisk the mixture for 3-4 minutes to thicken it. If you skip this step it will not set and if you beat it too long the toffee will harden too much. Spread the mixture over the bottom layer and place it in the fridge to harden.

3. Make the topping by melting the chocolate chips and remaining 2 tbsp of butter in a small pan over low heat, stirring continuously. Gently spread the melted chocolate over the top of the cooled toffee layer and allow the chocolate to cool and harden before serving.

Opposite: The hand-carved Bacchus fountain at Dirty Laundry Vineyard in Summerland

Drinks

Alcohol - the cause of and solution to all of life's problems.

Homer Simpson

Fort's Blackberry Sunrise

Featuring The Fort Wine Company's Isle Queen

This tasty twist on the Tequila Sunrise is an after-work favourite of the good folks at The Fort Wine Company. The drink replaces tequila with vodka and uses their blackberry port-style wine to add more colour and flavour into the mix.

Serves 1

INGREDIENTS

2 oz vodka

⅔ glass orange juice

2 oz blackberry port-style wine

1 dash grenadine

kiwi wedge for garnish (optional)

1. Fill a large wine glass with ice, add the vodka and top with orange juice.

2. Carefully pour in the port-style wine so that it runs down the inside of the glass and layers itself on the bottom. This is much easier to do if you have a pour spout on the bottle. Add a dash of grenadine and enjoy. This drink looks great garnished with a wedge of kiwi fruit.

Claret Cobbler

A Claret cobbler is almost like a traditional wine spritzer, but it is made with red wine and includes summer berries. Claret is the English name for wines from the Bordeaux region of France. In BC, wines made from the same types of grapes as Claret are often referred to as Meritage.

Serves 1

INGREDIENTS

½ cup red wine
1 tbsp triple sec (orange liqueur)
1 tsp sugar

¼ cup mixed summer berries
¼ cup soda water

1. In a mixing glass combine the wine, triple sec and sugar and stir well.

2. Fill a tall glass with berries and ice and pour the red wine mixture over top. Top the glass with soda water. Sip away and enjoy the summer.

Tropical Hibiscus Dream

This incredible concoction comes from mixologist Gavin Forbes of London's infamous Cuckoo Club. It uses hibiscus flowers to add fragrance and flavour to this original tropical cocktail. You can make hibiscus syrup by soaking 5 oz of dried hibiscus flowers in a bottle of gomme or sugar syrup for 2-3 days, until the syrup turns bright red. You can buy dried hibiscus flowers from a tea shop.

Serves 1

INGREDIENTS

½ cup white wine
1 tbsp lemon juice
¼ cup hibiscus syrup

3 tbsp pineapple juice
lemon-lime soda (eg. 7Up or Sprite)

1. Combine the wine, lemon juice, hibiscus syrup and pineapple juice in a cocktail shaker with ice. Shake well.

2. Pour the shaken mixture into a tall glass over ice and top with lemon-lime soda.

Christmas Glühwein

If you have ever been to a German Christmas market, it is likely that you have sampled some Glühwein. This mulled wine concoction will warm your cockles and put you in a festive mood regardless of the season. It is perfect for filling up a thermos and bringing to Christmas parties.

Serves 6

INGREDIENTS

15 cloves
1 lemon, halved
1 orange, halved
1½ cups water

½ cup sugar
3 cinnamon sticks
1 bottle red wine

1. Stick the cloves into the rind of the fruit. Combine the water, fruit, sugar and cinnamon sticks together in a saucepan and bring to a boil over medium-high heat. Reduce to a simmer for 25 minutes.

2. Add the wine, stir well, increase the heat and bring it almost to a boil. Reduce the heat before it reaches a boil. Keep the pot on the stove over low heat for 5 minutes. Remove and discard the solids before serving in mugs. Enjoy!

Vanilla Blanctini

Ahh the crisp flavours of Sauvignon Blanc mixed with vanilla vodka. Perfection in a glass. This cocktail is as simple as they come and it is great to come home to after one of those nightmare days at the office. The natural acidity of the Sauvignon Blanc contrasts nicely with the sweetness in the pineapple juice.

Serves 1

INGREDIENTS

2 oz vanilla vodka
2 oz Sauvignon Blanc

2 oz pineapple juice
dash fresh lime juice

1. Combine all of the ingredients in a cocktail shaker with ice and shake well.

2. Strain into a large martini glass and sip those office blues away.

Pomegranate Sangria

This modern version of a sangria uses pomegranate juice to make a delicious refreshment that is perfect for a warm summer's day. Make sure to prepare it well in advance so that the flavours have time to seep into the fruit.

Serves 8

INGREDIENTS

2 cups pomegranate juice
1 cup orange juice
1 bottle red wine
¼ cup vodka

1 orange, peeled and sliced
1 apple, cored and sliced
1 cup grapes, halved

1. Combine all of the ingredients together in a pitcher and mix well. Place in the fridge for 2-3 hours.

2. Serve the sangria in highball glasses over ice.

Mint Bubble Berries

This delicious concoction is perfect for celebrating special occasions, but then again, who really needs an excuse to spoil yourself? Use whatever berries are in season and the great thing about this drink is that it's easy to keep topping up your fruit-filled cup with more sparkling wine if you desire. The fruit will soak up lots of the delicious flavour from the sparkling wine so use a spoon to eat the berries at the end. Enjoy!

Serves 4-6

INGREDIENTS

1 cup halved strawberries
1 cup blueberries
1 cup raspberries

1 tbsp sugar
1 handful mint leaves, chopped
1 bottle chilled sparkling wine

1. In a bowl mix the berries together with the sugar and mint leaves.

2. Transfer the fruit to large martini glasses and top with the chilled sparkling wine.

Sumac Ridge Pink Grapefruit Mimosas

Featuring Sumac Ridge Steller's Jay

This is a refreshing alternative to the traditional Mimosa. Instead of orange juice, you use pink grapefruit juice which is attractive and delicious. The triple sec adds an extra boost, although you can leave it out if you want to keep the alcohol content down. The award-winning Steller's Jay was BC's first premium sparkling wine and it works perfectly with this lovely cocktail, which can be served at brunch, or any time of they day.

Serves 6

INGREDIENTS

1½ cups chilled pink grapefruit juice

½ cup triple sec (optional)

1 bottle chilled sparkling wine

pink grapefruit segments for garnish

1. Combine the grapefruit juice with the triple sec in a jug and stir. Pour evenly among 6 champagne flutes.

2. Top each flute with the sparkling wine and serve with a segment of pink grapefruit as a garnish.

Very Bloody Mary

The Bloody Mary and its Canadian cousin the Caesar are savoury cocktails that almost constitute a meal. Adding a touch of red wine to the mix is a trick employed by many professional bartenders who want to make their Bloody Mary the best in town. Now that we have revealed the secret, you too can create this gourmet version in the comfort of your own home. Also said to cure hangovers, a Very Bloody Mary may be just what the good doctor ordered after a night of indulgence.

Serves 1

INGREDIENTS

celery salt to rim the glass
2 oz vodka
6 oz tomato juice
½ tsp horseradish
1 tbsp red wine

2 tsp lemon juice
5 drops Tabasco (or to taste)
7 drops Worcestershire sauce
salt and freshly ground black pepper
1 rib celery

1. Prepare a tall glass by dipping the rim in a saucer of water and then celery salt and filling the glass with fresh ice cubes.

2. Combine the vodka, tomato juice, horseradish, wine, lemon juice, Tabasco, Worcestershire and salt and pepper to taste in a shaker with ice. Shake vigorously .

3. Strain the delicious concoction into the rimmed glass and garnish with a fresh rib of celery. Sip away and feel any traces of a hangover magically dissipate, but don't have too many or that hangover will be back the next day.

Wine Education

When it comes to wine, I tell people to throw away the vintage charts and invest in a corkscrew. The best way to learn about wine is the drinking.

Alexis Lichine 1913-1989

The Wine Grapes Of BC

One of the best things about BC wine is that there is so much variety in the types of wine available. Different wine grapes can produce completely different flavours, scents and characteristics in wine. The following is a rundown of some of the most common wine grape varietals that you are likely to encounter in BC, a brief summary of their history and some tips on the types of foods that they pair well with.

White Wine Grapes

Pinot Auxerrois Commonly shortened to Auxerrois, this grape can be traced back to the Alsace region of France, where it is commonly blended with Pinot Blanc.

It is believed that George Heiss of Gray Monk Winery first introduced the grape to British Columbia in the early 1970s. The grape is now widely planted in BC and some great success is coming from Vancouver Island as well as the Okanagan.

Pinot Auxerrois often displays aromas and flavours of apples, citrus and peaches and a musky aroma is sometimes present. It is fantastic for pairing with salads and it also goes very well with fish and poultry.

Some BC standouts of this varietal include Gray Monk, Gehringer Brothers, Little Straw and Zanatta.

Bacchus Named after the Roman god of wine, this varietal was originally created in Germany during the 1930s by crossing Müller Thurgau with a Silvaner-Riesling cross. The grape is now predominantly grown in Germany and the UK.

The grape is well suited to BC as it buds early and it grows successfully in some of the slightly cooler regions of the province. When it ripens fully, Bacchus can share some of the aromatic characteristics of Muscat or Riesling.

Some common aromas and flavours include citrus, apples, peaches and tropical fruit. A floral aroma is also often present. It is delicious paired with spicier dishes, such as Thai or Mexican cuisine. It is also well suited to white meats such as chicken or pork.

Some BC standouts of this varietal include Domaine de Chaberton, Arrowleaf, Larch Hills and Cherry Point.

Chardonnay Perhaps there is no other wine that inspires such a love/ hate relationship with wine drinkers as Chardonnay. Some wine drinkers even refer to themselves as *ABC drinkers* (Anything But Chardonnay).

The grape itself traces its origins to the Burgundy region of France. Even today, Chardonnay usually comes in a wide-bottomed "Burgundy" bottle, which is also used for Pinot Noir.

Chardonnay is the most widely planted white wine grape in BC with more than 700 acres in the ground. The Chardonnay grape usually ripens fairly early in the season and it can do well in cooler climates. It was Chardonnay that first put BC on the world wine map in 1994, when Mission Hill Winery won the top trophy at the London International Wine and Spirit Competition.

Chardonnay is commonly aged in oak barrels; however, beginning in the 1990s some winemakers started aging in stainless steel tanks to produce wines that reflect more of the grape's natural character.

Chardonnay is usually quite dry. Some common flavours include tropical fruit, apple, pineapple and citrus. When aged in oak, the scent of vanilla is often present. Chardonnay pairs well with lobster, shellfish, chicken and pork.

Some BC standouts of this varietal include Mission Hill, JoieFarm, Burrowing Owl and Crowsnest.

Chenin Blanc This varietal can be traced back to the Anjou region of France around the 9th century. It was one of the first varietals grown in South Africa, where it is also known as Steen, with the first plantings established in the mid-1600s.

In BC, Road 13 Winery makes an Old Vines Chenin Blanc from vines that are more than 40 years old. Although the grape has a long history in BC, it is not widely planted.

Some common characteristics of Chenin Blanc are a slightly floral nose and aromas and flavours of apricot, citrus and tropical fruit. It generally makes a wonderful sipping wine and it pairs well with herb-roasted chicken, simple seafood dishes and fruit platters.

Some BC standouts of this varietal include Road 13, Quails' Gate and Inniskillin.

Ehrenfelser Created at the famous Geisenheim Institute in Germany in 1929, this varietal is named after a 13th century castle on the Rhine River.

The varietal was introduced to BC by Walter Gehringer of Gehringer Brothers Winery in the late 1970s. It has thrived in BC and is more popular here than most places in the world.

The grape ripens earlier than Riesling and produces a delicious, aromatic wine. The usual wine style is off dry, although there are also some successful dessert wines made from this grape.

As a table wine it pairs very well with spicy Indian food, although it is also very popular as a picnic wine to accompany light, simple fare.

Some BC standouts of this varietal include Summerhill, CedarCreek, Gehringer Brothers and Lake Breeze.

Gewürztraminer The origins of this grape can be traced back to the Middle Ages in the German Alps. The grape is thought to have mutated from the Traminer grape some time in the last few centuries. "Gewürtz" is the German word for spicy and it is common for wines made from this varietal to have some spicy characteristics.

In BC, some of the oldest Gewürztraminer vines are the "Woo Woo Vines" owned by Dirty Laundry. These vines were planted back in the late 1970s.

Gewürztraminer grapes are usually a reddish-pink colour and often there is a pink tinge in wines made from this varietal.

Gewürztraminer comes in a variety of styles, but in BC off-dry seems to be the most common. It is very fragrant and common words used to describe the smell of these wines include "floral", "lychee" and "rose". It is excellent for pairing with spicy dishes and Asian cuisine. It is especially good with creamy Thai-style curries as the acidity cuts beautifully through the cream.

Some BC standouts of this varietal include Wild Goose, Thornhaven, Blasted Church and Dirty Laundry.

Kerner A cross between the Riesling and Trollinger grapes, this varietal was created in Germany in the late 1960s. The grape is named after a German poet from the 1800s and it is very popular in Germany and Italy.

Introduced to BC in the mid-1970s by George and Trudy Heiss of Gray Monk Winery, Kerner has proved itself as a very worthy addition to the BC wine scene and excellent examples are found all over the province.

The grapes are hardy and frost resistant and in many ways the wines are reminiscent of Riesling. They can have floral aromas as well as a green leafiness at times. Some common flavours include pear and citrus with a nice spiciness. They can also be made into delicious dessert wines.

Some BC standouts of this varietal include: Gray Monk, Oliver Twist and Tinhorn Creek.

Muscat The Muscat family, with more than 200 known sub-species, is one of the world's oldest varietals and scientists have proved that an alcoholic beverage made from Muscat grapes was served at the funeral of King Midas in ancient Crete!

Orange Muscat, Muscat Ottonel and Black Muscat, which makes a red wine, are some of the Muscat family grapes that are found in BC. These wines smell much like the grapes themselves; if you are in a vineyard with Muscat plantings, give them a good sniff. In AD 77, the ancient Roman Pliny declared the varietal "the grape of bees" because of its overpowering scent.

In much of the world, Muscat grapes are used to make dessert-style wines; however, in BC it is more commonly used to make off-dry table wine. Muscat is usually very food friendly and pairs well with seafood and Asian dishes.

Some BC standouts of this varietal include: Hillside Estate, Blue Grouse and Mistral.

Optima Created as a cool climate varietal during the 1970s, this grape has fallen from fashion in much of the world. In the late 1980s, the grape was widely planted in the Mosel region of Germany, but today the majority of those plantings have been replaced with other varietals.

The grape does well in BC, where it is mostly used for dessert-style wines. It ripens early and by leaving it on the vine it is perfect for sweet late harvest wines. Optima has common characteristics of tropical fruit and honey and it is fabulous served with cheese or fruit platters.

Some BC standouts of this varietal include: Quails' Gate, Recline Ridge and Lang.

Ortega This relatively new varietal was created in Bavaria in the early 1970s. It is a cross between Müller-Thurgeau and Siegerrebe. In Germany, it is known primarily as a blending grape and it is usually mixed with Riesling.

In BC, the grape has become a favourite of many local wine drinkers. Many feel that the best Ortega in the world is produced on Vancouver Island, where the grape has been growing since the early 1980s. However, as the varietal is popular throughout BC this is often disputed.

Ortega is usually aromatic with flowery notes and common characteristics include flavours and aromas of peach, apricot and citrus. It is a wonderful patio sipping wine and some great pairings include Cajun foods, fresh seafood, cheese platters and fruit salads.

Some BC standouts of this varietal include Starling Lane, Rocky Creek and Recline Ridge.

Pinot Blanc Sometimes unfairly referred to as "poor man's Chardonnay", Pinot Blanc is one of the shining stars of BC wine production. The grape itself is a mutation of Pinot Gris, which is thought to have originated in the Burgundy region of France. Today, the varietal is better known for its success in France's Alsace region.

Pinot Blanc has been popular in BC since the late 1970s. In much of the world it can be uninteresting; however, in BC the wines are lively and vibrant. Still, it seems that the varietal is losing popularity as more fashionable plantings take over.

Common characteristics of Pinot Blanc include aromas and flavours of apple, melon and pear. It can be oaked or unoaked, with the latter being especially suited to West Coast seafood. Some other great pairings are pork and poultry. It also makes an excellent aperitif with olives and cheese.

Some BC standouts of this varietal include Calona, Van Westen, Dunham & Froese and Blue Mountain.

Pinot Gris Also known as Pinot Grigio, Pinot Gris is a close relation to Pinot Noir. The name is a combination of the French words "Pinot", which means pine cone and "Gris", which means grey. It was derived because of the grape's colour and the resemblance of the grape cluster to a pine cone. Although, in BC the grapes are usually more of a purplish-blue kind of grey.

The grape was introduced to BC by George Heiss of Gray Monk Winery in Lake Country. Pinot Gris is now the third most popular varietal, after Chardonnay and Merlot, with more than 500 acres planted across BC and the wines are winning medals at competitions around the world.

Pinot Gris is at its best when consumed young and it can be either tangy and light or rich and full bodied depending on the ripeness of the grapes and the techniques used to make the wine. Traditionally, for a Pinot Grigio styled wine, the grapes would be harvested earlier and the wine would be lighter as a result.

Common characteristics of Pinot Gris include aromas and flavours of pear, apple and peach. It is great paired with seafood and with soft cheeses such as Brie or Camembert.

Some BC standouts of this varietal include Lake Breeze, Stoneboat, Averill Creek, River's Bend and Gray Monk.

Opposite: A bunch of Chardonnay grapes

Riesling The origins of this grape can be traced back more than 500 years to the Rhine and Mosel River Valley in Germany. German Rieslings are still often regarded as some of the best white wines in the world.

In BC, there are more than 250 acres of Riesling planted, with some of the oldest vines at Tantalus vineyards in Kelowna. These vines were planted in 1978 and are still producing fantastic wines.

In BC, during the 1970s right up until the late 1980s, there was a widely planted varietal called Okanagan Riesling, which had no relation to true Riesling. In the late 1980s, growers were paid by the government to rip this varietal, and several others, out to replace them with more premium varietals. Now quite rare, Okanagan Riesling can still be sampled at House of Rose Winery in Kelowna.

Riesling is one of the few white wines that age well and in Europe it can be very expensive. It is one of the last crops of the year to be harvested and Riesling, perhaps more than any other varietal, tends to pick up flavours in the vineyard; grapes grown in different soils can taste very different.

Riesling can be made in many styles, from very dry to very sweet and it also makes great Icewine. It is very aromatic and common scents include floral aromas, spice, apple, peach, honey and citrus. It pairs well with spicy Asian and Mexican cuisine and most seafood.

Some BC standouts include Tantalus, Orofino, 8th Generation and Pentâge.

Above: Riesling grapes ready to be harvested

Opposite: Court Faessler of River's Bend Winery at work in the vineyard

Wine Education

Sauvignon Blanc The popularity of this varietal has soared in the past few years. Although its original home is the Loire River Valley area in France, it is the crisp wines of New Zealand that have recently been capturing headlines (and gold medals) around the world.

Fortunately, the climate in BC is equally suitable for producing world-class Sauvignon Blanc. Although the grape first appeared in BC during the 1970s, it was completely wiped out by frosts in the 1980s, only to make a welcome return in the 1990s. Its popularity has continued to rise and it is now an important staple for many wineries.

The wine is famous for its herbaceous grassy characteristics and common flavours often include grapefruit, melon and even figs and bananas. Some wonderful food pairings include seafood, chicken, goat cheese, salads and almost any dish that uses red peppers.

Some BC standouts of this varietal include Stag's Hollow, Little Straw and Jackson-Triggs.

Semillon Traditionally, Semillon has been blended with Sauvignon Blanc to make the famous dry white wines of Bordeaux. In recent times, this grape has been experiencing a resurgence. At one time, it is believed that Semillon was the world's most widely planted wine grape. Even today, plantings can be found across the globe in countries such as Israel, Portugal, Tunisia, South Africa, Chile, Argentina and Australia.

The grape ripens earlier than most and is thick skinned, which means it is less susceptible to frosts, an important factor in BC. Some common characteristics of Semillon include floral aromas and flavours of pear, figs and peach. The wine is delicious paired with roast chicken and turkey, Caesar salad and creamy pastas.

Some BC standouts of this varietal include Mt. Boucherie, Lake Breeze and Township 7.

Vidal Also called Vidal Blanc in other parts of the world, historians believe that the varietal was created in Europe during the 1930s. It hasn't been popular in Europe, but has proved to be very successful in North America.

It is through Icewine that the Vidal grape shines because of its thick skin and winter hardiness. As an Icewine, Vidal has been a winner at many prestigious competitions around the world including the Grand Prix d'Honneur at Vinexpo in Bordeaux.

Vidal Icewines often have characteristics of orange zest, marmalade, citrus, baked apple and honey. It is fantastic as a dessert on its own, or it pairs very nicely with blue cheese. As a table wine, more grapefruit tends to show and it is excellent paired with cheeses, poultry dishes and salads.

Some BC standouts of this varietal include Prospect Winery, Inniskillin, Golden Beaver and Arrowleaf.

Viognier Often touted as "the next Chardonnay", Viognier has well and truly landed on the BC wine scene. The grape's origins are somewhat unclear and some wine historians claim that the grape can be traced right back to the Roman Empire. By the 1960s, there were only a few hectares of this varietal left in the world and they were planted in the Rhone Valley. Since then, it has been saved from extinction with large plantings now distributed around the world.

The grape is quite new to BC and its popularity is already leading to increased production. Viognier is also used as a blending grape for red wines.

Some common characteristics of Viognier are scents and flavours of peaches and apricot. It pairs exceptionally well with spring vegetables, poultry dishes, mushrooms, creamy pasta and risotto. It is also wonderful with soft cheeses and fruit platters.

Some BC standouts of this varietal include Silk Scarf, Golden Beaver and La Frenz.

Jeff Martin, the winemaker at La Frenz on the Naramata Bench.

Red Wine Grapes

Baco Noir There is very little Baco Noir growing in BC and most Canadian plantings of this varietal are found in Ontario. Like Marechal Foch, the grape is sometimes looked down upon because it is a hybrid of North American and European varietals. However, when treated with care, this varietal can create delicious, complex and highly sought after wines.

The grape is an early ripener and is very winter hardy. The wines it produces are dark and smoky and often have flavours and aromas of blackberries, dark chocolate, earth and coffee. The wines are excellent when paired with roasted red meats, pizza and even dark chocolate.

A BC standout of this varietal is Summerhill.

Cabernet Franc DNA testing has confirmed that Cabernet Franc is actually one of the parent grapes of Cabernet Sauvignon. It is one of the prized red wine varietals of Bordeaux. Although it still ranks behind Merlot and Cabernet Sauvignon in popularity, it is increasingly common to see this varietal turned into a wine in its own right.

One of the most successful Cabernet Franc plantings in the province is at Burrowing Owl and numerous awards have been won by the winery for this varietal. In BC, Cabernet Franc has also been successfully turned into Icewine.

Cabernet Franc tends to have less tannins and more acid than Cabernet Sauvignon, and the grapes are thinner skinned and ripen earlier. This is a varietal with fairly good aging potential and common flavours and aromas include blueberry, cherry, blackcurrant and sometimes coffee, leather or a slight smokiness. It's popular with vegetarians because it pairs well with hearty vegetables such as zucchini, squash and carrot and it is a big hit with vegetarian lasagne. It also pairs well with steak, lamb and tuna.

Some BC standouts of this varietal include Burrowing Owl, Hester Creek, Quinta Ferreira and Sumac Ridge.

Cabernet Sauvignon The history of this varietal can be traced back about 600 years to the vineyards of Bordeaux, France. It is actually a cross between Cabernet Franc and Sauvignon Blanc.

This varietal has been very popular in BC and there are now more than 500 acres planted. Most of these vines are found in the Southern Okanagan as this region has the best climate for these grapes. One of the oldest and most successful Cabernet Sauvignon plantings is in the Dark Horse Vineyard planted by Inniskillin's winemaker Sandor Mayer. Wines coming specifically from this vineyard are usually sold under a special label.

One of the great things about Cabernet Sauvignon is that it is wonderful for aging and often the best wines will benefit from laying down for 5-10 years. Through this aging process, the wines pick up flavours and aromas of cedar and leather and the tannins found in the wine become much smoother.

Cabernet Sauvignon often has aromas of blackcurrant and dark berry fruits. It can also have notes of mint, green pepper or even eucalyptus. It pairs very well with steak, dark meats and duck, as well as rich meat and tomato based pasta sauces. It goes well with with dark chocolate or aged cheeses.

Some BC standouts of this varietal include CedarCreek, Road 13, Nk'Mip Cellars, Fairview Cellars and Peller Estates.

Cabernet Sauvignon grapes on the vine

Gamay Noir In 1395, Phillip the Bold, Duke of Normandy, ordered that all Gamay Noir vines be ripped from the ground in Burgundy and that Pinot Noir be planted in its place. Fortunately for us, in nearby Beaujolais there were no such rulings, and from there the grape has spread around the world.

In BC, Gamay Noir can be made in very different styles. Often it is light and tangy, but it can also be made into a darker medium-bodied wine. It is one of the first varietals to bud and flower and often it is one of the first red wines to hit the stores, as most feel that it is best when consumed young.

Gamay Noir often has flavours of cherry, strawberry and raspberry and it sometimes has a pungent earthiness present on the nose. It's great for barbecues and sometimes shows better when served slightly chilled.

Some BC standouts of this varietal include Desert Hills, Granite Creek, St. Hubertus and Poplar Grove's Monster Vineyards.

Malbec A fairly new addition to BC's repertoire of wines, Malbec is an overwhelming success with great wines being produced by several wineries. The grape is one of those permitted in Bordeaux blends, but it's most famous for its presence in Argentina, where it was introduced in the late 1800s. Today, many of the world's best Malbecs are said to come from Argentina.

In BC, Howard Soon of Sandhill was the first to create a single-varietal wine from Malbec, using grapes harvested from the Phantom Creek Vineyard in 2001. Today, more and more producers are planting Malbec as its popularity increases with the public.

Malbec is usually very dark and inky in colour and often has flavours and aromas of plum and blackberry. It is usually medium to full bodied and tends to pair well with lamb, steak and rich tomato-based pasta dishes.

Some BC standouts of this varietal include Inniskillin, Sandhill, Kettle Valley and Red Rooster.

Marechal Foch This grape was created by French Hybridizer Eugene Kuhlman and named after the French WWI General Ferdinand Foch. It has become something of a cult grape in BC, despite the majority of Foch plantings being pulled up during the 1980s.

The vines are hardy and produce a high tonnage. Quails' Gate in West Kelowna has some old vines Marechal Foch and they produce a bold, dark wine. Ex-Quails' Gate winemaker Jeff Martin (now at La Frenz Winery) is often credited with bringing Marechal Foch back into fashion in Canada.

Marechal Foch is often described as having gamey, meaty or earthy aromas and flavours of blackberry, cassis, dark chocolate and coffee. It is a wine that some people love and others despise. It pairs well with game meats, duck, lamb or even cigars!

Some BC standouts of this varietal include Quails' Gate, Alderlea and Lang.

The sandy desert soils of Osoyoos are perfect for growing flavourful wine grapes

183

Merlot The origins of the Merlot grape can be traced right back to the 1st century in France. It is one of the famous Bordeaux varietals and the world's most sought after (and expensive) Merlots still come from this area. A bottle of the famous Chateau Petrus usually costs $1,000-$2,000 US.

In BC, Merlot was first planted in the 1970s and those original vines are owned by CedarCreek Winery. There are now around 1,000 acres of Merlot planted in BC.

Merlot grapes are larger and mature earlier than Cabernet Sauvignon grapes. For long term cellaring, the wine is at its best when blended. One of the reasons that Merlot is so popular is that it produces delicious full-flavoured red wines that can be consumed young, without having to wait for the aging process. The wine is often described as soft, lush and as having a velvety mouthfeel.

Some common characteristics of Merlot are scents of plum, blackcurrant, cherry, vanilla and cloves. It pairs very well with lamb, grilled meats, game, hearty tomato-based pastas and aged cheeses.

Some BC standouts of this varietal include Nk'Mip Cellars, Tinhorn Creek, Kettle Valley and Church & State.

Petit Verdot This varietal has garnered interest in BC, mainly due to the popularity of Meritage wines (Bordeaux blends). It is one of the varietals allowed in the blends, but it is usually only added in small quantities. The name translates to "little green" and it was probably called this because it is one of the last grapes of the season to ripen. Because of this, with Petit Verdot, perhaps more than any other varietal, different years may produce very different results with some years resulting in no harvest at all.

Howard Soon of Sandhill Winery made BC's first single-varietal Petit Verdot with grapes harvested in 2002 and the wine was released to excellent reviews.

Petit Verdot grapes are small and thick skinned and they produce dark peppery wines that can be high in tannins. Common characteristics can include flavours and aromas of blackberry, cherry, leather and dark chocolate. Some great wine pairings include lamb, prime rib, pepper steak and strong cheeses.

Some BC standouts of this varietal are Sandhill and Inniskillin. Most wineries growing this varietal use it only in blends.

Opposite: A bunch of Pinot Noir during harvest